THE TWENTIETH-CENTURY WORLD

TEACHERS' RESOURCE BOOK

Other Special Needs Support Material

Medieval Realms Special Needs
  Picture Pack ISBN 0–7195–5382–2
  Picture Pack Workbook ISBN 0–7195–7056–5 (single)
                      ISBN 0–7195–7057–3 (pack of 5)
  Teachers' Resource Book ISBN 0–7195–5381–4

The Making of the UK
  Picture Pack ISBN 0–7195–7044–1
  Picture Pack Workbook ISBN 0–7195–7226–6 (single)
                      ISBN 0–7195–7233–9 (pack of 5)
  Teachers' Resource Book ISBN 0–7195–7043–3

Peace & War
  Pupils' Book ISBN 0–7195–4977–9
  Teachers' Resource Book ISBN 0–7195–4978–7

Britain 1750–1900
  Picture Pack ISBN 0–7195–7046–8
  Picture Pack Workbook ISBN 0–7195–7227–4 (single)
                      ISBN 0–7195–7234–7 (pack of 5)
  Teachers' Resource Book ISBN 0–7195–7045–X

DISCOVERING THE PAST

**SPECIAL NEEDS
SUPPORT MATERIALS**

THE TWENTIETH-CENTURY WORLD

TEACHERS' RESOURCE BOOK

COLIN SHEPHARD   ANN MOORE

JOHN MURRAY

Acknowledgements

The authors and publishers would like to thank all the schools which trialled these materials.

Photographs are reproduced by courtesy of: Hulton Getty (pp.82, 84 bottom, 126, 144 top, 173), Mary Evans Picture Library (pp.84 top and middle, 145 left), The Fawcett Library/Mary Evans Picture Library (pp.91 bottom, 93), The British Library (p.86), Imperial War Museum (pp.90, 91 top left, top right and middle, 136, 150), Popperfoto (pp.142, 144 bottom, 145 right, 146 left), 146 right, Professor Walter Hege* (p.166), Victor Weisz 'Vicky', Evening Standard/Centre for the Study of Cartoons and Caricature, University of Kent at Canterbury (p.207).

Every effort has been made to contact copyright holders, and the publishers apologise for any omissions which they will be pleased to rectify at the earliest opportunity.

First published 1997
by John Murray (Publishers) Ltd
50 Albemarle Street
London W1X 4BD

Illustrations by Jeff Edwards, Janek Matysiak, Ann Moore

Layouts by Amanda Hawkes

Typeset in 14/18pt Quorum Book by Wearset, Boldon, Tyne and Wear
Printed and bound in Great Britain by St Edmundsbury Press, Bury St Edmunds

A CIP catalogue record for this book is available from the British Library.

ISBN 0–7195–7047–6

THE SCHOOLS HISTORY PROJECT

This project was set up by the Schools Council in 1972. Its main aim was to suggest suitable objectives for history teachers, and to promote the use of appropriate materials and teaching methods for their realisation. This involved a reconsideration of the nature of history and its relevance in secondary schools, the design of a syllabus framework which shows the uses of history in the teaching of adolescents, and the setting up of appropriate examinations.

Since 1978 the project has been based at Trinity and All Saints' College, Leeds. It is now self-funding and with the advent of the National Curriculum it has expanded its publications to provide courses for Key Stage 3, and for a range of GCSE and A level syllabuses. The project provides INSET for all aspects of National Curriculum, GCSE and A level history, and also publishes *Discoveries*, a journal for history teachers.

Enquiries about the project, INSET and *Discoveries* should be addressed to the Schools History Project, Trinity and All Saints' College, Brownberrie Lane, Horsforth, Leeds LS18 5HD.

Enquiries about the *Discovering the Past* series should be addressed to the publishers, John Murray.

Series consultants
Terry Fiehn
Tim Lomas
Martin and Jenny Tucker

Contents

Introduction

All too often the history diet offered to pupils with special needs has consisted of crosswords, word-searches and 'gap-filling'. SHP's special needs support materials, on the other hand, have been developed to meet a specific demand from schools for materials that have all the hallmarks of SHP's 'real history' approach – in which pupils investigate issues and explore sources for themselves, and reach their own conclusions – but which at the same time recognise the very real problems some pupils have with the language of written source material and the unstructured nature of some historical tasks.

These materials have been developed by a team of writers and special needs advisers. They have also been trialled in a number of schools around the country. The result is a set of flexible and innovative strategies which aim to:

- motivate pupils to find out about the twentieth-century world, by developing their historical skills and understanding at an appropriate level
- give all pupils access to this important core unit
- add variety to the teaching of **The Twentieth-Century World**.

The materials consist of this Teachers' Resource Book, with more than 200 photocopiable pages, and a companion Picture Pack, which contains 24 full-colour, large-size, pictorial sources, together with a wide range of suggested activities using the pictures. The Picture Pack activities can be photocopied from the accompanying teachers' notes, or a separate workbook is available. All in all, these materials provide several 'pathways' through **The Twentieth-Century World** which will suit a wide range of classroom situations.

The three pathways

- Pathway 1 is for pupils who have severe difficulties with reading. Through the Picture Pack they can receive a 'minimum entitlement' **The Twentieth-Century World** unit – through the use of pictorial source material alone.
- Pathway 2 is for lower-achieving pupils who can, nonetheless, cope with a certain amount of carefully targeted reading and writing. The Picture Pack and the differentiated worksheets, games and stories in this accompanying Teachers' Resource Book together provide a flexible alternative to using a class textbook. Indeed, this pathway can operate independently of any textbook and does not require users to have classroom sets of SHP's **The Twentieth-Century World** unit.
- Pathway 3. In classes where SHP's *Peace & War* is being used as the classroom textbook, the Picture Pack and the Teachers' Resource Book provide a wide range of materials to support slower learners and reluctant readers, by simplifying written source material and giving structure for pupils' written responses to questions in the textbook.

Main features of the support materials

These support materials respond to a number of the important requirements of low-attaining pupils:

Motivation

- In common with the entire *Discovering the Past* series, the main aim of the support materials is to help pupils of all abilities to realise how fascinating history can be and to enjoy participating in history lessons.
- The course is founded on the belief that pupils of all abilities can cope with investigation of real historical issues as long as they are presented at an appropriate level.
- The materials aim to give pupils a high success rate – to increase motivation by ensuring positive achievement.

Differentiation

- While the materials in SHP's **The Twentieth-Century World** unit are demonstrably capable of differentiation 'by outcome', there is often a need to differentiate 'by task'. Used alongside the core unit, these materials vastly increase the opportunities for differentiating pupils' work in Y9. The detailed teachers' notes which follow indicate many ways in which further differentiation can be achieved.

General learning skills

- The materials encourage a variety of methods of learning.
- They also aim to involve pupils in decisions about their learning, making them aware of the learning objectives and helping them to recognise what progress they are making.

Minimum entitlement

- The authors have defined a minimum entitlement for **The Twentieth-Century World** with three main elements: an overview and two depth studies. The choice of depth study will obviously be affected by whether pupils are progressing to GCSE and if so which syllabus they are taking.

Language skills

- The support materials have not been written to a single formula – nor have they been written at a single level. Instead, the language level of the authors' text, the written sources and the tasks has been carefully monitored to ensure it is totally suited to the nature of the material and the learning context of the pupils. For example, in certain tasks where group learning is being encouraged and pupils can gain support from their peers, a higher level of language is deemed appropriate than where pupils are working independently.

■ The materials are designed to complement the language policy of the school in a number of ways:
  – by enhancing pupils' general reading skills
  – by developing pupils' subject-specific vocabulary (through the use of a feature called 'History Dictionary')
  – by developing higher-order reading skills, such as text interrogation and cross-referencing skills
  – by ensuring that pupils' writing tasks are always undertaken for a purpose and for a good range of purposes
  – by providing plentiful opportunities for group discussion.

Using these support materials

In this book you will find over 200 photocopiable worksheets which cover key aspects of the programme of study for **The Twentieth-Century World**.

■ **An overview**: this is tackled through the Picture Pack and personalised through focusing on two families: the O'Connors of Liverpool and the Oppenheimers of Nuremberg. The same families also appear where appropriate in the depth studies in the Teachers' Resource Book, so with careful planning you can grow your depth studies out of the overview.

■ **Depth studies** on:
  1. The First World War (Tasks 6–13)
  2. How did women win the right to vote? (Tasks 14–17)
  3. The rise of the dictators in Europe (Tasks 18 and 19)
  4. Hitler's rise to power (Tasks 20–24)
  5. The Home Front in the Second World War (Tasks 25–31)
  6. The Holocaust: what was it and why did it happen? (Tasks 32–37)

■ **Conclusion**: this focuses on the end of the war and the legacy of the war (Tasks 38–41).

■ **Cross-unit work**: as the final volume of KS3 Special Needs Support Material, this volume includes an appendix using all the different Picture Packs for cross-unit work (Tasks 42–45).

Planning your course

There are two main ways to use these materials.

1. They can be used as a self-standing course. We have covered the main areas of the programme of study for **The Twentieth-Century World** and all the key elements of the unit. The activities are self-contained in that all the sources and resources you need to run the activities are provided for you in the Teachers' Resource Book and in the companion Picture Pack. There is no requirement that you have stocks of *Peace & War* or any other textbook. These materials can provide you with a worksheet-based course which can be used alongside any textbook or none.

2. They can equally well be used to support the use of SHP's **The Twentieth-Century World** unit in schools which are already using *Peace & War*. The aim has been to make selected enquiries more accessible to those with learning difficulties. This has been achieved by:
  ■ giving additional structure for pupils' tasks
  ■ narrowing the selection of source material for pupils to work with
  ■ further simplifying the language of the written sources
  ■ providing much bigger visuals for the pupils to work with (in the Picture Pack)
  ■ helping teachers to identify where pupils need help in making progress in history.

This book provides differentiated materials which enable pupils with learning difficulties to examine the same issues and tackle the same enquiries as mainstream pupils using *Peace & War*. It allows them to develop their understanding of the same historical concepts as the rest of the class, but at their own pace and to their own level. And as their understanding grows, some pupils will be able to move confidently from support materials to textbook – choosing to work on the tasks in *Peace & War* in preference to the tasks in this book.

Trialling experience has shown that in practice these materials are immensely flexible and that they can also provide invaluable support for pupils of a much wider range of abilities than simply those with learning difficulties. In some schools, tasks such as 20 (on the reactions to the Treaty of Versailles) or 32 (on the background to anti-Semitism in Europe) have proved useful as a starting point for entire classes, leading them into the relevant enquiries in *Peace & War*.

Progression

With this volume the first phase of SHP's special needs provision for Key Stage 3 is now completed. The full suite of resources is summarised at the beginning of this book.

The four units have been planned to provide opportunities for progression across Key Stage 3; cross-unit work becomes an important feature in later units. It is therefore advised that you also purchase copies of the resources for earlier units if you have not already done so.

Differentiation

Differentiation is about helping pupils to progress at their own speed – hardly a novel idea. Yet the word sometimes fills people with fear, maybe because it has become the focus of recent criticism by OFSTED inspectors.

The problem is, of course, that all pupils are different, yet are usually taught together in groups of about thirty. How can teachers help each of them to progress at his/her own pace? These materials will offer you a practical set of strategies for achieving differentiation in your history teaching. However, some preliminary words of caution are needed. Discussion about differentiation is too often hampered by the assumption that it simply involves giving pupils different work to do. This obscures the fact that if pupils are to make progress then some more basic aspects of good practice are important. These following aspects of good practice have formed the bedrock of the strategies in the support materials:

1. <u>Making aims and objectives clear</u> We have tried to set clear aims and objectives and to help pupils understand what these are. The detailed notes which follow describe the aims of each task. We would encourage you always to talk with pupils about what is being done and why. This applies both on the overall level of planning a route through the unit (see page 5), and at the level of the individual exercise.

2. <u>Making objectives achievable</u> We have tried to ensure that these tasks can be tackled at a range of levels. Only you will know what is really achievable with your individual pupils – so we have tried to give you plenty of opportunities to set specific, itemised, achievable objectives for each pupil. (See also the notes on the Special Needs Code of Practice on page 5.)

3. <u>Monitoring and assessing the progress the pupils are making</u> If pupils are to make progress, formative assessment is essential and these materials offer plentiful opportunity for you to make your own written, narrative comments on pupils' work. These comments should identify and praise achievement but also provide signposts for future work. Talking with pupils about their work and encouraging self-assessment – by allowing them to select pieces of their own work to display in a portfolio – is an effective way of encouraging progress.

4. <u>Building on what the pupils already understand and re-applying skills and understanding in a new context</u> In rough terms about 80 per cent of what takes place in a lesson should be consolidating what has already been achieved in terms of skills and understanding. About 20 per cent should involve setting pupils new challenges or introducing new ideas. If you go any faster you will risk losing many pupils; if you go more slowly, they may be bored through a lack of challenge. Throughout this material we have therefore introduced new content and ideas gradually, step-by-step, and offered regular opportunities for pupils to revisit skills and concepts in a new context.

5. <u>Using a variety of teaching and learning styles</u> Pupils are best motivated by the use of a range of learning situations and teaching methods. These materials can give them the experience of whole class work, small group work, work in pairs and individual work. There are opportunities for discussion as well as writing, drawing, matching, sequencing and source interrogation. One should not underestimate the power of the well-told story in history teaching. Story therefore forms the backbone of pupils' work on both the Home Front and the Holocaust.

6. <u>Encouraging pupils to experiment and take risks</u> We have avoided activities which deal mostly in 'right and wrong' answers. They lead to pupils becoming discouraged. They will avoid participating because of the fear of making mistakes. We have preferred to use open questions and problem-solving enquiries where all genuine efforts can be praised. By encouraging group work and allowing pupils to work in small groups with others of similar ability it should be possible, with careful planning, for each pupil to make a valuable contribution to the overall group effort.

The most essential factor in differentiation remains the role of the teacher in the classroom. Many teachers will offer appropriate support to pupils of different abilities as a matter of course. This can take various forms. It is worth your considering how effectively this is done in your own department. Teachers will often rephrase explanations and instructions for the whole class. Extra explanation and support will be given to individual pupils as the teacher walks around the classroom discussing the work. During these discussions teachers might provide more structure for some pupils or reduce the demands by helping with the first few steps of the work. They might point individual pupils towards other resources which will help them with their work.

There will never be just one correct approach to differentiation, and effective differentiation cannot be achieved overnight. You will constantly need to adapt and adjust your teaching methods and your presentation of activities to allow individual pupils to progress. The bulk of the detailed notes on pages 13–21 is concerned with the matter of how to achieve further differentiation for individual pupils by varying the input and support given, by providing additional structure for an answer, and by asking pupils to respond in different ways.

A sample worksheet

Header shows the number of worksheet pages needed to do this task, and 'You will need' lists other materials pupils will need to complete the activity. These features help put pupils more effectively in control of their own learning.

'History Dictionary box'
Whenever necessary this book provides the support pupils need in order to understand subject-specific vocabulary *before* they meet the word in the worksheet.

Worksheet title

Introductory text
This is kept to the minimum necessary to introduce the task. Further background information and help with contextualising the task are provided in the detailed teachers' notes for you to use if you think it necessary.

'Your task'
- This is presented to a standard format.
- Stages in a task are numbered clearly.
- An adequate space is left for pupils to write or draw their own answers on this sheet if required.

Icons indicate the nature of the task.

📖 reading

✏️ writing or drawing

✂️ cutting

📑 sequencing or matching

💬 discussion

🎲 game

🔍 look closely

There are three pages to this task

34

You will need
- pen or pencil
- a set of cards showing anti-Semitic laws
- some sheets of A3 paper
- felt-tipped pens

◆ HISTORY DICTIONARY	My explanation of them
The important words	
Nuremberg Laws	
synagogue	

What did Hitler do to the Jews in Germany during the 1930s?

Adolf Hitler became Chancellor of Germany in 1933. Soon he began to persecute the Jews. One Jewish man remembers how they all felt. 'Everybody shook. As kids of ten we shook.'

Hans Oppenheimer was extremely worried. He and his family were now living in Berlin, the capital of Germany. In 1935, Hitler passed a set of laws called the **Nuremberg Laws**. These meant that Jews lost all their rights as German citizens. This was just too much for Hans. He found another job in Holland and soon his wife, the two boys, both sets of grandparents and a new baby called Eve were living near Amsterdam in Holland.

Back in Germany, the persecution of the Jews gradually got worse. Slowly, but surely, all their rights and freedoms were taken away. (The photograph opposite shows Nazis pasting signs on a Jewish shop window to persuade people not to buy goods from them). On 9 November 1938, all over Germany, Nazi stormtroopers broke into and smashed up tens of thousands of Jewish shops, homes and **synagogues** (the buildings where Jews hold their religious meetings). In many places, ordinary Germans joined in and helped the stormtroopers. This night became known as *Kristallnacht* or the 'night of glass'.

Your task 📖 💬 ✏️
You should work in pairs for this task.
1. Read Source 1 on page 2. It describes what happened to the Jews who were arrested on *Kristallnacht*.
2. Read the words on page 2. They describe the actions of the stormtroopers. With your partner, decide which word is the best description? Which word is the next best, etc?
3. Complete the statements on page 2.

© JOHN MURRAY   THE TWENTIETH-CENTURY WORLD SUPPORT MATERIALS

173

The Code of Practice on Special Educational Needs

Working together to enable children with a range of needs to learn effectively has always been recognised as good educational practice. 'It presents teachers with some of the most challenging and rewarding work the education service can offer.' (Code of Practice on Special Educational Needs 1994)

Every school's special needs policy now reflects the 'Staged Response to Learning Needs' which was outlined in the 1994 Code of Practice, and all teachers are expected to demonstrate how they differentiate children's learning experiences to meet these needs. **The Twentieth-Century World** support materials have been written to enable teachers to plan learning experiences which cover a wide range of learning needs and which can link both directly and indirectly with the core textbook.

Planning for Stage 1 of the 'Staged Response to Learning Needs'

There are several stages of learning need for which teachers now have to plan (see fig. 1). Most children with special needs are within the first stage. Their understanding and enjoyment of history will grow through using **The Twentieth-Century World** support materials as a stimulus for more in-depth work from a textbook (whichever this may be). They will also make progress as a result of the time teachers always invest in quality discussion and explanation with children who are learning more slowly.

When planning history for these children, teachers will be able to use their normal schemes of work, highlighting or underlining the planned activities and resources which have been differentiated for those children within Stage 1. The blank matrix on page 7 will be a useful tool in such planning. Teachers could also record in their class register which children fall into this category so that it is clear at whom the differentiated planning has been targeted.

Planning for Stages 2 and 3

For those children whose learning needs are more complex and who fall within Stages 2 and 3, planning, monitoring and evaluation intensify. The Special Needs Co-ordinator and possibly the Support Services will be involved. **The Twentieth-Century World** materials have been designed to present achievable targets for these children too. The matrix on page 7 (see the *Medieval Realms Support Materials Teachers' Resource Book* for an example of its use) enables teachers to set targets for pupils who have been identified as having general learning difficulties. These targets would normally be agreed upon with the Special Needs Co-ordinator, the support teacher and, where appropriate, the child him/herself. The targets

for Stages 2 and 3 are a focus of particular attention at OFSTED inspections.

Children's individual entitlement

We are all aware that learning does not always progress in a clear linear fashion, and children do not always remain conveniently within the stages provided by the Code of Practice! However, these support materials, in defining the minimum entitlement for each topic, and in providing differentiated tasks, provide a framework within which children can progress at a rate which suits their individual learning needs.

Stage 1: **Class or subject teachers** identify or register a child's special educational needs and, consulting the school's SEN Co-ordinator, take initial action.

Stage 2: The school's **SEN Co-ordinator** takes the lead responsibility for gathering information and for co-ordinating the child's special educational provision, working with the child's teachers.

Stage 3: Teachers and the SEN Co-ordinator are supported by **specialists from outside the school**.

Stage 4: **The LEA** considers the need for a statutory assessment and, if appropriate, makes a multidisciplinary assessment.

Stage 5: **The LEA** considers the need for a statement of special educational needs and, if appropriate, makes a statement and arranges, monitors and reviews provision.

Schools and LEAs will need to be able to demonstrate, in their arrangements for children with special educational needs, that they are fulfilling their statutory duty to have regard for this code. In the case of schools, OFSTED and OHMCI (Wales) inspection teams will consider the effectiveness of schools' policies and practices and the extent to which schools have had regard for the code.

Fig. 1 Stages of Provision

Practical considerations
Preparation

Many of the tasks do require a certain amount of preparation. We have attempted to highlight in the detailed notes where there is a particular need for this. However, here are a few general points to bear in mind.

For activities such as Tasks 19, 30 and 34 you can enlarge pictures, captions and text before cutting them out. Mounting these on thin card and laminating them extends their shelf life and means less preparation the following year!

There are some 'resource sheets' – e.g. family cards for Task 2 – which need copying on to card of different colours.

Most of the tasks have more than one page. You can give the sheets out one by one. Occasionally the later sheets in the task are 'extension sheets' only, to be available if a pupil asks for them.

If you are planning to use the 'History Dictionary' feature, you will need to photocopy the definitions on pages 227–230 on to card.

The teaching environment

Don't forget how much the teaching environment can help pupils. The walls of the classroom are a potential resource if you cover them with helpful illustrations, charts, diagrams and timelines to which pupils can refer.

Reference material (e.g. the History Dictionary file – see page 9) should be readily available.

Pupil folders

There are obvious benefits in pupils creating a folder in which to store their completed drawings, written answers, worksheets, and their larger pieces of work.

To give extra coherence and status to this file, there is a photocopiable 'title page' for pupils to personalise for the front of their folders (see page 10). In the centre pupils should stick in or draw a picture which they feel expresses something important about the period. It is worth spending time over this and perhaps turning it into a discussion activity in which pupils compare and talk about the pictures they have chosen.

There are also two photocopiable templates (lined for written work and unlined for artwork), both with attractive borders and spaces for pupils to write in their names, the date and the topic. Hopefully these will encourage pupils to take pride in their work. You will find these templates on pages 11 and 12 of this book.

Teachers could encourage pupils to think in terms of constructing their own history book.

The rationale behind pupils using their own workbook together with the Picture Pack is similarly for them to feel that their work has status and permanence.

'My pathway through The Twentieth-Century World'

An important part of ensuring motivation is setting appropriate achievable targets and allowing pupils to monitor their own progress against these targets (see above under 'Differentiation'). The photocopiable planning sheet on page 8 is designed to help teacher and pupil plan together and record progress. Pupils should fill in this chart in discussion with their teacher. They can then decorate it and add it to their folder. It should also be copied for your own records. Use and adapt the sheet however you wish. We envisage that the numbered lines will list the most important tasks pupils are going to tackle.

Timelines

All pupils need a chronological framework, not just those with learning difficulties. It would be useful to have the following two timelines prepared:

1. A horizontal timeline spanning around 5000 years, with the names of different eras, and in relevant sections dating by centuries. You could use frieze paper or wallpaper for this. You should already have this if you have used the **Medieval Realms** support materials.
   Whenever pupils are being introduced to a new study unit or are revising their skills of chronology, they should look at this timeline. It is important that they are helped gradually to develop an understanding of where, in general terms, **The Twentieth-Century World** stands in relation to, e.g. **Britain 1750–1900** or even, from KS2, **The Victorians**.

2. The other timeline should be for the period the class is studying; in this case 1900 to the present. This should be on as large a scale as possible – dating by decades is ideal. The timeline could be mounted on sugar paper or wallpaper lining and pinned to the wall.
   As well as dates, give it shape by adding pictures of the main events and people.
   Pupils can add to the timeline as their knowledge and understanding of the period increase.
   It could be useful to divide the timeline up into parallel sections – one row each for Britain and Germany with a third row for wider developments. Each section can be colour-coded and added to as and when the need arises.

Year 9 History   Unit:

Name of pupil

....

....

General target

Support planned

Specific target for this lesson

Content	Vocabulary	Key questions	Historical skills and concepts	Teaching and learning activity	Resources

My pathway through
The Twentieth-Century World

Name _____

Term _____

Subjects to be investigated	Date completed
Overview: _____	_____
1. _____	_____
2. _____	_____
3. _____	_____
Depth study 1: _____	_____
1. _____	_____
2. _____	_____
3. _____	_____
Depth study 2: _____	_____
1. _____	_____
2. _____	_____
3. _____	_____
Conclusion: _____	_____
1. _____	_____
2. _____	_____
3. _____	_____

The History Dictionary

Throughout their study of history, pupils will come across strange and unfamiliar vocabulary. One recommendation of this course is that pupils compile their own history dictionaries. They could do this for each study unit.

This dictionary can be either a small (indexed) book – such as you can buy very cheaply in a stationers – or it can be a set of sheets in the back of pupils' **The Twentieth-Century World** folders.

Each time pupils come across an unknown or important new word, they should be encouraged to record it in their own dictionary – and they can also illustrate it if they wish.

Throughout the tasks in this book, new words are introduced and explained. The key ones, including the 'prescribed terms' identified for KS3 by the National Curriculum, are included in a History Dictionary box on the title page of each depth study or at the head of the worksheet. A definition can be given by the teacher or worked out by the pupil. Teachers should remind pupils to transfer these words and concepts into their own 'History Dictionaries'.

To help pupils who wish to write their own definitions, we have provided a photocopiable set of definitions of the key terms (pages 227–230). These can be photocopied on to card and kept available in a file in the classroom for pupils to consult when they are writing their definitions.

The dictionary definitions can also be used in other ways. For example, you can give pupils two or three definitions and ask them to find pictorial sources in the textbook or in the Picture Book to illustrate them.

The Picture Pack

The Picture Pack forms an essential part of this bank of resources. It contains full-colour, laminated images at large size, some chosen from *Peace & War*, and others entirely new pictures which extend the range of visual sources and can be used for comparative work.

Experience has shown that some pupils find it easier still to work with black and white outline drawings of these sources – because these can simplify some of the detail of the original image, and be used for pupils to label and mark. Outlines of all the images can be found on pages 231–246 of this book.

Stories

There are many stories in this TRB and the associated Picture Pack notes. There are various ways of using such stories, as explained in earlier volumes of the support materials. For example, you can: put the story on tape; photocopy the pictures separately and use them as a storyboard; white out picture captions – getting pupils to write their own; white out sections of the story – pupils write the missing sentence or paragraph; cut up and sequence the story; ask pupils to add their own illustrations for other moments of the story.

In this volume, however, there are stories which need particularly careful handling. For example, we have deliberately and understandably chosen not to illustrate the harrowing stories of Regina Franks and Paul Oppenheimer in the death camps (Tasks 35 and 36). This may seem to make the stories less accessible than earlier narratives. This is of course one form of progression, but if the stories are too difficult or demanding for your poorer readers we would recommend the option of putting the stories on to tape. If you could use a single storyteller for all Paul Oppenheimer's narratives that would further help pupils identify with it.

THE TWENTIETH-CENTURY WORLD

Name _____ **Class** _____

Year _____ **School** _____

Name _____

Date _____

Topic _____

Name _____

Date _____

Topic _____

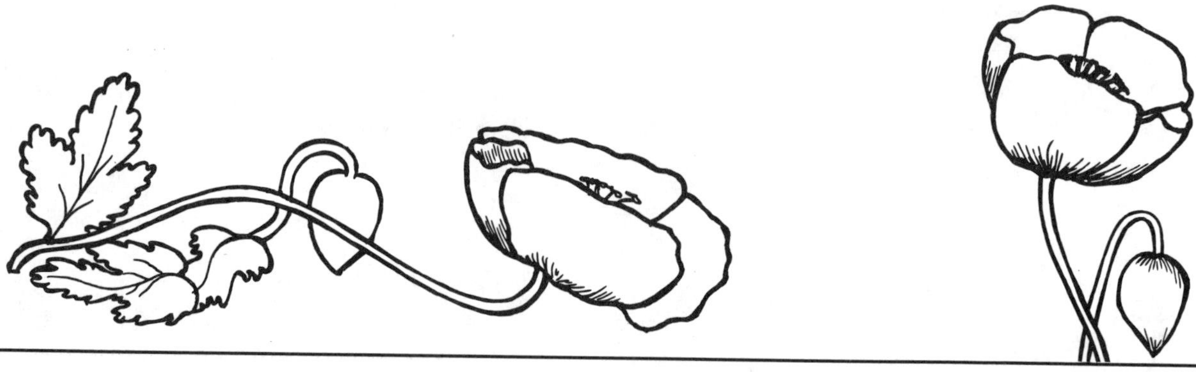

_____

_____

_____

_____

_____

_____

_____

_____

_____

_____

_____

_____

_____

Detailed teachers' notes

The aims of the detailed notes are:

- to put the most important events, etc. into a chronological framework
- to give pupils an overview of the twentieth century
- to enable pupils to develop further independent research skills.

To show how each extension relates to the key activity, we have used the following symbols:

↗ indicates steps beyond the key activity, involving higher-order skills

↔ indicates activities and approaches at a similar level

↙ indicates steps leading towards the key activity, or extension activities at a less complex level.

Overview: The twentieth-century world

Aim: to increase pupils' knowledge and understanding of the lives of ordinary people during the twentieth century so that they can begin to understand how the events and actions of politicians and other leaders affected everybody's lives.

Introduction:

↔ Pupils read introduction and do discussion task as set.

↔ Each person in the class writes down what he/she thinks the historian meant. These are discussed and mounted for display.

Task 1: What do you already know about the twentieth century?

Aim: to provide pupils with a chronological overview of the twentieth century.

Your task A:

↙ Hand out only one set of cards at a time, i.e. only famous people, or events or new technology.

↙ Pupils complete task A and, rather than write the events in chronological order, they glue the cards into place to make their own twentieth-century timeline OR they are given a photocopy of a completed timeline.

Your task B:

↗ Research on other famous people/events, etc. including the requirement to write about half a side of A4 describing what has been investigated. This can be read out to the rest of the class or form part of the group's wall display.

Task 2: Two twentieth-century families: the O'Connors and the Oppenheimers

Aim: to introduce pupils in overview to the O'Connor and Oppenheimer families through whose eyes they will view events of the twentieth century.

Your task:

↔ In some schools, there might be pupils who would like to bring their own family history into the unit. They could be encouraged to complete a similar family tree and to pursue ongoing investigations along similar lines for their families. This area needs to be treated sensitively by teachers.

Task 3: The O'Connors of Liverpool

Aim: to find out more detail of the life of the O'Connors before the War and to help pupils understand what daily life was like in Britain for many people at the time of the First World War.

(page 1)
Your task:

↙ Pupils only have to record the differences between then and now.

↙ Have a set of ready-prepared cards recording the differences between then and now. Pupils' first task is to sort them chronologically (i.e. use them as triggers for remembering the story). Then they have to decide which are the most significant differences and why.

↙ Read the story out to pupils. Every time they think a difference is mentioned they put their hands up. The differences are discussed and recorded on the board. Pupils 'copy them up' later.

↔ Where applicable, pupils are encouraged to investigate their own family origins from this period. They could bring in photographs (which you should photocopy) and other documents to go towards a class display.

↗ A possible homework task would be to find out about the fashions of the early 1900s and to prepare a small display about them.

↔ Pupils have to make a list of all the different types of evidence that could have been available to the author when she was researching the two family histories.

(page 6)
Your task:

↔ Take each object and decide which room it would have been found in.

↔ Take each object and decide who might have used it.

↔ Take each object and decide whether it was used by a servant or a family member.

↗ From what you have read about the O'Connors prepare a brochure advertising your local museum of social history, which features an ordinary family from the Edwardian era.

Task 4: Shopping: then and now

Aim: for pupils to compare shopping in 1917 with their own experiences of shopping nowadays.

(page 3)
Your task:

→ Do your own research about the price of houses, cars, clothes, etc. (Pupils always want to know!) Construct a similar activity comparing the two sets of figures.

Task 5: The Oppenheimers of Nuremberg in Germany

Aim: to encourage pupils to recognise that ordinary people in Germany were just as badly affected by the events of the twentieth century as people were in Great Britain.

Your task:

↙ Pupils take each drawing in turn. They label the 'clues' which tell them that the Oppenheimers were very wealthy. This is followed by a class discussion about the differences between the O'Connors and the Oppenheimers.

Depth Study 1: The First World War

Aim: to help pupils to understand that there were many complex causes for the First World War, some of which were short term and others long term.

To help pupils to organise their work and thinking to be able to write a short essay on the causes of the First World War.

Task 6: Why were Germany and Britain getting ready for war?

Aim: for pupils to understand the relationship between Britain and Germany, and to realise that their rivalry was one of the important long-term causes of the War.

Your task:

↙ Take images of the German Kaiser and British King and label their reasons for being suspicious of each other round the outside of their images.

Task 7: Which alliance was stronger?

Aim: for pupils to compare the relative strengths of the Triple Alliance and the Triple Entente, and to consider how the alliance system contributed to the outbreak of the First World War.

(page 1)
Your task:

↙ Give pupils the completed chart so that they can move straight into answering the questions about the individual countries.

(page 3)
Your task:

↗ Pupils write a paragraph explaining their views on whether or not the European countries should have been suspicious of each other.

Task 8: What events triggered the First World War?

Aim: to look at the short-term causes of the First World War, i.e. the events which triggered the start of the War.

Your task:

↗ Get pupils to do the activity on page 113 of *Peace & War* (The Stage is Set for War). Use this as a further preparation for writing the essay about the causes of the War.

Task 9: What were the causes of the First World War?

Aim: to enable pupils to write an essay about the causes of the First World War, differentiating between long-term and short-term causes, and recognising the most important causes.

Your task:

↙ Prepare a set of cards with the causes, both long- and short-term, of the War already written. Ask pupils to sort them and put them in order of priority before they start writing. The essay is a recording of these causes with support from you to link sentences and paragraphs together.

Task 10: What was trench warfare?

Aim: to investigate the nature of trench warfare.

(page 3)
Your task A:

↗ Give pupils some more verses of the poem and ask them to write a more 'in-depth' analysis of the poet's feelings.

↗ Pupils write their own poem about the futility of war.

Task 11: Who fought in the trenches?

Aim: to make pupils aware that people from all over Britain's Empire fought and died in the British Army during the First World War.

Your task:

↗ Pupils research their own family history to find out whether or not they have ancestors who were killed in the Great War. They begin to compile a Year Group file on those who 'Loved and were loved . . .'

→ Hold a class discussion on the role played by soldiers from the different parts of Britain's Empire.

How does this long history of loyalty tie in with the racist view that British citizens from different parts of the Empire who came to settle and live in Britain were/are scroungers?

Task 12: Telegrams from the trenches: an activity

Aim: for pupils to empathise with a soldier serving on the Western Front. The game describes the terrible conditions soldiers faced in the trenches.

Your task:

 Play the game but don't use the Diary Record cards. Simply follow the other instructions. At the end of the game pupils choose five or six of the different descriptions to write their own description of life in the trenches.

 Do the Activity on page 115 of *Peace & War* (A new kind of warfare).

Task 13: A comic-strip war

Aim: for pupils to examine and evaluate different sources of information about life in the trenches.

Depth Study 2: How did women win the right to vote?

Aim: to increase pupils' knowledge and understanding of the struggle for equality.

To complete the work on the Franchise, begun in the previous unit, **Britain 1750–1900**.

Task 14: Have there been any famous women in history?

Aim: to get pupils thinking about why the actions of women through history have received less attention from historians than the actions of men and to increase their knowledge of some famous women.

(page 1)
Your task:

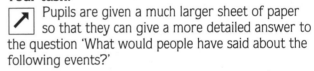 Once pupils have collated all the names of famous men and women, they research their dates, etc. This leads to a whole-class timeline of famous men and women.

Pupils move on to investigate why they were famous. Was it social, political, economic or cultural reasons? They record their findings and organise their lists accordingly.

(page 2)
Your task:

Introduce the cartoon as a piece of evidence. Initiate a class discussion as to the nature of bias and the usefulness of cartoons to the historian.

(page 3)
Your task:

Match up the information and picture cards. Ask pupils just to sequence them on to the timeline.

Task 15: How did the Suffragettes try to win the vote for women?

Aim: for pupils to examine the role played by the Suffragettes in the campaign for female suffrage.

You could use this quite detailed text to begin teaching pupils how to make notes from text.

(page 2)
Your task:

Pupils are encouraged to research more sources of information and to categorise them into those which tell them WHO, those which tell them WHAT, and those which tell them WHAT HAPPENED.

(page 6)
Your task:

Pupils are given a much larger sheet of paper so that they can give a more detailed answer to the question 'What would people have said about the following events?'

(page 7)
Your task:

Pupils work in groups of four and are given one article to write between them. Each person in the group is therefore only responsible for writing about one of the four 'questions'.

The newspaper article is a good vehicle for IT across the curriculum.

Task 16: Why did women's jobs change during the First World War?

Aim: to look at the way the First World War changed women's roles.

(page 3)
Your task:

Pupils only have to complete the middle set of boxes.

Task 17: Why did women get the vote in 1918?

Aim: for pupils to evaluate the reasons why women finally won the vote, by using information from different sources.

Your task:

Lead the discussions, taking each source in turn. The results of the class discussions are recorded on the board and pupils 'copy up' the work at the end of the lesson.

Depth Study 3: The rise of the dictators in Europe

Aim: to focus on how things changed as a result of global warfare.

To examine the roles of different individuals during the twentieth century.

To begin to understand key concepts which have shaped Western society.

Task 18: How are democracies and dictatorships different?

Aim: for pupils to understand how dictatorships and democracies work, and the main differences between them.

Your task:

✔ Give pupils fewer statements.

Task 19: Who were the European dictators?

Aim: for pupils to study and assess the political beliefs and actions of Hitler, Mussolini and Stalin. This will help pupils to understand why these three leaders were all dictators.

NB Teachers need to be aware that the speeches are imaginary.

(page 2)
Your task:

 Pupils are given enlarged map icons on separate cards so that they are having to sift through a variety of different types of information.

(page 3)
Your task:

✔ Sort out two of the files so that pupils, working in pairs, only have the documents relating to one dictator to sort out.

(page 4)
Your task A and B:

↗ Pupils bypass the Confidential Report sheet and move straight on to completing the Political Record sheet.

↗ Pupils are given a Political Record sheet, together with page references for information about each of the dictators. Instead of using the imagined speeches which are a compilation of each dictator's ideals, they investigate and research each dictator on their own, before completing the Political Record sheet.

Depth Study 4: Hitler's rise to power

Aim: to help pupils to understand how Hitler was able to persuade the German people to follow him.

To show what life was like for an ordinary German family living through the 'inter-war years' so that pupils can make comparisons between life in Germany and life in Great Britain.

To enable pupils to begin to collaborate and share information about Hitler's Germany.

Task 20: Why was the Treaty of Versailles so unpopular in Germany?

Aim: for pupils to appreciate that the terms of the Treaty of Versailles were viewed very differently by British and German people, and to assess how fair the treaty was.

Your task:

↙ You could write down the thoughts of British and German people about the terms of the treaty on a separate sheet of paper. Pupils have to decide which column each thought would belong in, i.e. was this a German thought or a British thought?

↗ Pupils move on to do questions 1 and 2 on page 117 of *Peace & War*.

Task 21: What was life like in Germany in 1923?

(*P&W* pp.120–121)

Aim: for pupils to imagine how ordinary Germans may have felt about the problems Germany was facing in 1923.

Your task:

✔ Cut out each envelope as a flashcard. Ask pupils to sort them chronologically.

↙ Pupils don't do the extra mathematics involved in working out the cost of sausages and bread. Tell them the answers so that they can move on to the empathetic reconstruction exercise.

Task 22: How did Hitler become Chancellor in 1933?

Aim: for pupils to understand how events in Germany during the 1920s and early 1930s led to widespread support for Adolf Hitler and his political beliefs.

Your task:

↗ Make sure that the more able pupils use the timeline of events in Germany. You could also give them photocopies of the relevant sources from *Peace & War* so that they have the information 'on tap'.

↗ Individual pupils are given both activities to do on their own.

✔ Make a set of cards with the answers to the questions written on them. Pupils are given the questions and answers on separate pieces of card. They match the correct answer to each question.

Task 23: Why did Hitler rise to power? Using the evidence

(*P&W* pp.120–121)

Aim: to reinforce the link between Germany's economic problems and Hitler's rise to power.

Your task:

↔ This particular exercise is a useful common assessment task for Year 9 pupils. Whilst some of the questions demand fairly straightforward answers, others require a higher level of understanding. You therefore can differentiate by outcome if you devise a workable mark scheme.

↗ Pupils move on to do question 1 on page 121 of *Peace & War*.

↗ The discussion question 'Why was Adolf Hitler allowed to become Chancellor of Germany?' is set as a homework essay.

Task 24: How did Hitler gain control of most of Europe, 1936–1941?

Aim: to give pupils an overview of the causes of the Second World War.

(page 1)
Your task:

↙ Cut up the comic strip (on page 2) and get pupils to sort the boxes chronologically before moving on to the set task.

(page 3)
Your task:

↗ Pupils work in groups of four. They take on the role of one of the four teenagers. Each pupil spends ten minutes preparing his/her thoughts. Then sitting round a table, they debate the following question:
   'Is Adolf Hitler justified in taking over France, Holland and Belgium?'

↗ Pupils move on to do the Activity on page 149 of *Peace & War*.

Depth Study 5: The Home Front in the Second World War

Aim: for pupils to understand what life was like during the Second World War for ordinary British families and to be able to compare their experiences with those of the persecuted minorities in the rest of Europe.

Task 25: Living through the War 1939–1945: The O'Connor family preparing for the worst: September 1939

Aim: to look at the way ordinary people responded to the outbreak of war and what preparations were made against bombing raids.

(page 2)
Your task:

↙ Record the correct answers in each box, cut up the pictures and boxes and give them to pupils to match.

↙ Give pupils only two or three pictures to guess at.

↗ Pupils record the right reasons and then, working in groups, decide which were the most important reasons and which were the least important.

↗ Pupils write a paragraph explaining why some cities were important targets for German bombers.

↗ Ask pupils to discuss the question 'Would the British Air Force use the same tactics on German cities?'

(page 3)
Your task:

↙ Divide pupils into groups. Each group shares its ideas about the gas attack leaflet and records its answers on only one leaflet.

Task 26: Evacuation: we're going to the country

(*P&W* pp.153–157)

Aim: for pupils to appreciate how difficult evacuation must have been, both for young children and teenagers sent away from their families to a strange place and for host families who took evacuees into their homes.

Your task:

↗ Pupils move on to do the Activity on page 153 of *Peace & War*.

(page 3)
Your task:

↗ Read the story out to the class. Pupils compose a short play where they re-enact the 'drama' but give it a different ending. Perhaps the Welfare Officer turns up after all? What will she have to say to Frank about his behaviour? Perhaps Mr Davies comes home and decides on a suitable punishment, etc?

↗ Pupils go home and (where appropriate) interview their own grandparents or someone they know about their experiences of being evacuated. They bring their evidence to the next lesson. Comparisons are made. What are the similarities and differences between various sets of memories?

↗ Pupils move on to choose some of the Activities on pages 154–157 of *Peace & War*.

Task 27: The Blitz begins

(*P&W* pp.164–165)

Aim: to give pupils some idea of the horrific consequences of the Blitz.

Your task:

☑ Divide pupils into groups of four. Each person in the group reads Source 1 and looks for evidence of one of the four statements.

↔ Discuss the powerful message of the source. Did pupils realise just how badly many people suffered in the War?

↗ Pupils read the sources on pages 164–165 of *Peace & War*. They complete the second part of the Activity, i.e. 'Write down five entries from the diary of a Civil Defence worker for September 1940.'

Task 28: Keeping up morale

(*P&W* pp.166–167)

Aim: for pupils to understand why the government controlled information and imposed censorship during the War.

Your task:

☑ Give pupils only two of the four sources to interpret.

↗ Pupils discuss the question on page 167 of *Peace & War*, 'Why do you think it is difficult for historians to know what it was really like during the Blitz?'

Task 29: Women at work

(*P&W* pp.168–169)

Aim: for pupils to recognise that during the War thousands of women successfully took on work that they had never done before.

Your task:

☑ Pupils are given fewer sources to work with.

↗ Lead a discussion: 'What are the similarities between women's work in the First World War and women's work in the Second World War?' Record the results of the discussion on the board for pupils to note in their books or folders.

↗ You could also discuss the question: 'How far, if at all, had attitudes TO women **and** the attitudes OF women changed in the intervening twenty-five years?'

↗ Pupils move on to answer questions 2–5 on page 169 of *Peace & War*.

Task 30: Rationing

(*P&W* pp.170–171)

Aim: to examine the effects of wartime rationing in Britain. The game describes how one family may have tried to get extra food or new clothes for a special occasion.

(page 3)
Your task:

↗ Pupils move on to complete some of the Activities on page 171 of *Peace & War*.

Task 31: How did people in Britain and Germany feel about the War?

Aim: for pupils to be aware how the events of the War were interpreted differently in Germany and Britain.

(page 1)
Your task:

☑ Pupils are given significantly fewer timeline events to deal with.

☑ The events are cut into strips first of all so that pupils have to do a sorting exercise, and therefore have to read about each event carefully.

↗ Some of the British or German responses are blanked out so that pupils write in their own 'propaganda responses'.

↗ Pupils move on to do question 1 on page 150 of *Peace & War*.

↗ Pupils prepare an outline history of the Second World War suitable for nine-year-olds, using the information from these timeline strips. They use their IT skills and can illustrate it appropriately.

Depth Study 6: The Holocaust: what was it and why did it happen?

Aim: to give pupils a detailed knowledge and understanding of the most horrific genocide ever perpetrated.

To enable pupils to realise that anti-Semitism was and is a worldwide problem, not just a German attitude.

To make pupils realise that in the roots of anti-Semitism lie the roots of all intolerance and bigotry, especially racism.

To fill pupils with a determination never to let something like the Holocaust ever happen again.

Task 32: Was anti-Semitism common in Europe?

(*P&W* p.186)

Aim: to look at the history of anti-Semitism over hundreds of years so that pupils are aware of the background to anti-Semitism in Nazi Germany.

Your task:

↗ Use your own background knowledge to give pupils further examples of anti-Semitic activity, particularly if any work has been done on other eastern European countries.

↗ Pupils research further evidence of anti-Semitic pogroms to compile a dossier.

Task 33: How did the Nazis stir up hatred against the Jews?
(*P&W* p.187)

Aim: to examine the methods used by Nazis in anti-Jewish propaganda.

(page 3)
↗ Page 3 is an extension sheet for users of *Peace & War* which allows two very different images to be compared.

(page 4)
↗ Page 4 attempts to stimulate pupil discussion of ways of identifying and countering racism and prejudice which will necessarily form the backdrop for the historical work on the Holocaust which will be undertaken over the next 30 pages.

Task 34: What did Hitler do to the Jews in Germany during the 1930s?
(*P&W* pp.187–188)

Aim: for pupils to understand how Hitler intensified persecution of the Jews during the 1930s and early 1940s, first by organising violent attacks such as *Kristallnacht* and then by making anti-Semitic laws which gradually deprived every Jewish man, woman and child of all basic rights.

(page 3)
Your task:
↙ Give pupils the Jewish restrictions posters one by one. They record their feelings about each restriction.

↗ Pupils try to imagine they are the parents of young Jewish teenagers who are already banned from German schools and have encountered many other restrictions. How will they persuade their children to obey every new restriction as it is imposed?
Set up a role-play situation in which the restrictions are introduced.

Task 35: What did Hitler do to the Jews of Europe during the Second World War?
(*P&W* pp.188–193)

Aim: for pupils to learn about the terrible conditions in which Jews lived in the ghettos and the systematic policy of genocide carried out by the Nazi death squads and in the concentration camps.

Your task:
↙ Divide the class into three groups. Each group takes one of the ways in which Hitler murdered the Jews. They do the tasks set in Stages 1, 2 and 3

but also compose a talk about what they have found out. A spokesperson delivers this talk to the rest of the class.
↗ Pupils compose a letter from Regina to her mother. Mrs Frank was writing a note for Regina as she was led away by the German guards. Regina was always certain that the note told her to 'Stay alive so that you can tell the world about the evil of the death camps'. What will Regina tell her dead mother?
↗ Ask pupils to describe the feelings of the young woman as she held her baby up to the guards and asked them to save it (see page 6).

Task 36: How did the Oppenheimers suffer during the Holocaust?

Aim: for pupils to empathise with the Oppenheimer children in Bergen-Belsen.

Your task :
↙ Focused listening. Ask pupils, as they hear the story, to note what happens to one chosen character.

Task 37: Why did so many Jews starve in the death camps?

Aim: for pupils to realise how little food the children were given in the camp and to compare it with the diet of an average teenager nowadays.

Conclusion: How did the Second World War end?

Aim: for pupils to begin to understand the complex nature of causation and how, if people were unaware of the likely consequences, decisions could be made which, with the benefit of hindsight would be deemed inappropriate.

Task 38: Why did the USA drop the atomic bomb and what were the consequences of it?
(*P&W* pp.198–201)

Aim: for pupils to examine the principal causes and consequences of the first atomic bomb.

Your task A:
↙ Provide the consequence sources one by one to pupils so that they are not overloaded. Pupils tackle as many as they can in the time available.
↔ Pupils record consequences on separate cards. Using these cards they work in pairs, moving them up and around the table until they can come to some agreement as to which were the most/least important consequences of the bomb.

(page 4)
Your task:

 Pupils are given these questions to answer in written form.

 Pupils move on to answer questions 1–3 of the Activity on page 201 of *Peace & War*.

Task 39: Technology, transport and two world wars

Aim: to develop pupils' research and referencing skills, and to investigate the impact of two world wars on technology.

Your task:

✔ Ask pupils to work with only a few of the invention cards.

✔ Hold a class discussion to record how and why these inventions helped in wartime.

Task 40: Looking back on the twentieth-century world

Aim: for pupils to compile their own overview of the events they have studied in **The Twentieth-Century World**.

(page 1)
Your task:

✔ Pupils could be given just one category to work on.

Task 41: How have our towns and cities changed?

Aim: for pupils to examine the way in which cities have changed over the twentieth century, and what factors have most influenced change.

(page 1)
Your task:

 Pupils can be given just the developments: they can write their own results.

✔ You could select just three developments and three results for pupils to match.

(page 2)
Your task:

If you have the Picture Pack for *Britain 1750–1900* you will find a full-colour version of the 1900 town scene in there. Use it to introduce this task.

✔ Pupils can work with Picture Source 16 to help them in drawing their own present-day picture. It is important that they do not simply copy Picture Source 16, or if they do copy details from it, that they still make an attempt at explaining the changes they have decided to show.

Appendix: Cross-unit work for all at Key Stage 3

The final tasks (42–45) form a review of Key Stage 3 using the four picture packs for:

■ **Medieval Realms**
■ **The Making of the UK**
■ **Britain 1750–1900**
■ **The Twentieth-Century World**

and other resources.

Task 42: 1000 years of change

Aim: to compare twentieth-century change with changes in earlier periods that pupils will have studied.

You will need the four picture packs, or equivalent pictures from other books showing cities through the period.

Your task:

This is an open-ended task which can easily be adapted to the aptitude of your pupils by:

✔ Providing pre-selected pictures or half completed explanations.

 Taking away the 'categories' and allowing pupils a free choice.

↔ The display could be a pre-determined class display into which they are fitting their own feature.

✔ Pupils could be asked to compare only the beginning and end of the period, missing out the middle stages.

✔ Pupils could be asked to work solely with a series of four town pictures i.e.: Picture Sources 15 and 16 from *Making of the UK*, 1 and 2 from *Britain 1750–1900* and 16 from *The Twentieth-Century World*.

Task 43: Gathering evidence

Aim: to look at 1000 years of Key Stage 3 history to think about the differences between different kinds of history: political, economic, social and cultural.

Your task:

✔ As for Task 42, carefully pre-selecting from the Picture Sources can provide further support for the most able.

✔ The words political, economic, social and cultural history could be omitted, and instead the meanings as in the preamble to the task substituted, e.g. evidence about how leaders ruled their country; how people made a living; how people lived in their homes; how they enjoyed themselves.

Task 44: When would you like to have lived?

Aim: for pupils to explain which period of those they have studied in Key Stage 3 would have been the best or worst time to live.

This task is for pupils to do alone. It forms a good basis for completing Task 45.

Task 45: Comparing periods: 1066 to the present

Aim: to build on the previous task by looking in greater depth at the character of each of the periods as revealed by visual evidence.

This task forms a class activity.

Your task:

This task, more than any other in the Appendix, lends itself to the use of a much wider range of evidence: textbooks, reference books, CD Rom, etc. The extended writing work which could develop from this is rich and varied.

OVERVIEW
The twentieth-century world

♦ HISTORY DICTIONARY

The important words	My explanation of them
technology	_____
	_____
communications	_____
	_____

Introduction

During the next few years people will look back on the twentieth century. They will talk about the good things that happened such as the National Health Service, old-age pensions and cures for many diseases. They will think about the major changes that took place in **technology** and **communications**. They will 'surf the Internet' and discuss these changes with people from every part of the globe.

There will be radio and television programmes about famous twentieth-century events such as the first man on the moon, or Britain getting its first woman Prime Minister. Finally, they will remember famous people like Mother Teresa, Nelson Mandela and Mahatma Gandhi.

People will also talk about the bad things: the wars, famine, unemployment, racism, drugs and violence. They may argue about who was the most evil person of the twentieth century. Was it Adolf Hitler or Josef Stalin, or even Fred West?

Like all periods of history, there are events to find out about, people to investigate, changes to examine and lessons to be learned. A famous historian once said: 'Those who do not learn the lessons of history are doomed to relive it.'

 What do you think the historian meant?

1

You will need
- scissors
- pen or pencil

What do you already know about the twentieth century?

Your task A

Your teacher will give you a set of cards.

1. Cut out all the cards.
2. Sort them into three piles:
   - ■ A = cards about famous people
   - ■ B = cards about important events
   - ■ C = cards about new technology.
3. Sort each pile into chronological order.
4. In your exercise book (or folder), write down the events from pile B in chronological order.
5. Choose one card. Use an encyclopaedia to find out some more details about the person, event or new piece of technology. Record these details on a sheet of paper to put on a whole-class timeline.

> **Using your own background knowledge, can you spot any links between certain people, events, or new technology?**

Your task B

Your class should divide into three groups.

1. Each group chooses one of the categories: people; events; technology.
2. Using the library, CD Rom and other reference materials, find out about other famous people or events or new technology of the twentieth century.
3. Design a large poster for display that contains all the information you have researched in your chosen category.

>
> - ■ How will you try to organise your information so that it makes sense?
> - ■ Will it be recorded chronologically?
> - ■ Will you include some drawings?
> - ■ How much will you write?
> - ■ How will you make sure you're not just copying?

☞

A   Famous people

Cut out the cards below to complete task A on page 1.

✂

1917
Vladimir Ilich Ulyanov (Lenin) started the Communist Revolution in Russia.

1993
Nelson Mandela became the first Black president of South Africa.

1979
Margaret Thatcher became the first woman Prime Minister of Great Britain.

1948
Mahatma Ghandi freed India from British rule.

1939
Adolf Hitler was the German leader who caused the Second World War.

1930
Amy Johnson flew solo to Australia.

1903
Emmeline Pankhurst formed the Suffragettes who wanted votes for women.

1990
Benazir Bhutto became the first woman Prime Minister of Pakistan.

1945
Winston Churchill led Britain to victory against Germany in the Second World War.

1968
Martin Luther King was murdered because he was trying to get equal rights for Black people in America.

B   Main events

Cut out the cards below to complete task A on page 1.

1914–1918
First World War
Eleven million people died as soldiers from all over the world fought in the War.

1986
Chernobyl disaster
A nuclear reactor exploded in Russia. Hundreds of thousands of people got radiation poisoning.

1939–1945
Second World War
This was a war to stop Adolf Hitler from taking over all of Europe.

1945
First atomic bomb dropped
The Americans dropped the biggest bomb ever on Japan.

1941
The Holocaust
Hitler wanted to kill all the Jews in Germany and in the other countries he conquered. He built gas chambers so 2000 Jews could be murdered at a time.

1991
War in Bosnia
A terrible civil war began. It was caused by religious and ethnic hatred.

1969
First man on the moon
Three American astronauts landed on the moon.

1953
First man to climb Mount Everest
A group of British men climbed to the top of the highest mountain in the world.

1970 18-year-olds allowed to vote in Britain
18-year-olds were given the same rights as everyone else and could vote in elections.

10

1917
The Russian Revolution
A group called the Communists started a rebellion. They threw out the Russian Tsar (Emperor) and took over the country.

C New technology

Cut out the cards below to complete task A on page 1.

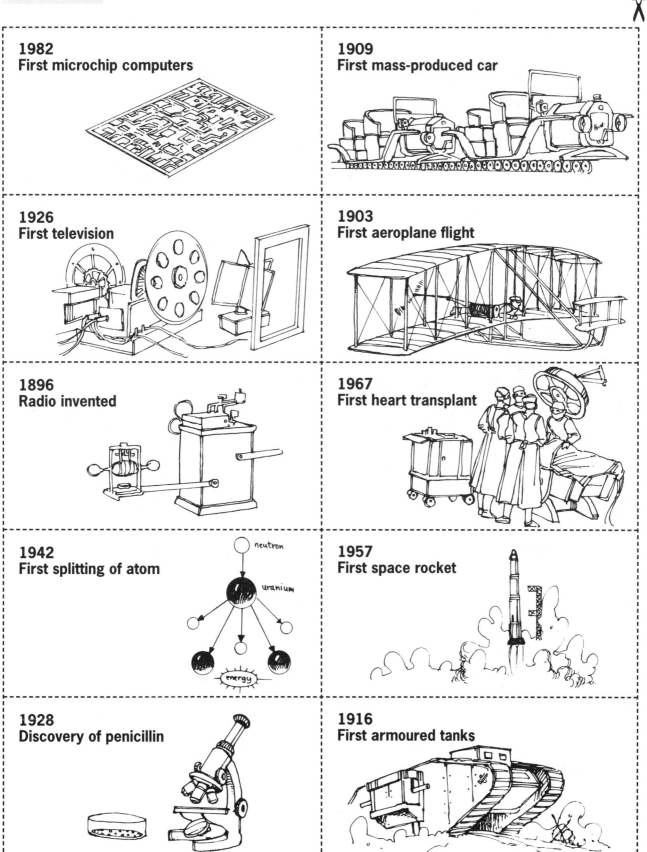

1982
First microchip computers

1909
First mass-produced car

1926
First television

1903
First aeroplane flight

1896
Radio invented

1967
First heart transplant

1942
First splitting of atom

neutron
uranium
energy

1957
First space rocket

1928
Discovery of penicillin

1916
First armoured tanks

2

You will need

- cards of the two families
- two family trees
- pen or pencil

Two twentieth-century families: the O'Connors and the Oppenheimers

---

◆ **HISTORY DICTIONARY**

The important words	My explanation of them
generation	_____
	_____
	_____

Introduction

As you study the twentieth-century world, you will find out what happened to two different families. Both families went through two world wars. One family, the O'Connors from Liverpool, was very lucky. The entire family survived the wars. The other family, the Oppenheimers from Nuremberg in Germany, was not so lucky. More than half of this family died during the Second World War.

Your task

You should work in pairs for this task.

1. Sort the family cards into two piles, one for the O'Connor family and one for the Oppenheimer family.

2. Place the oldest **generation** of each family at the top of your desk, then the next and so on. The youngest generation will be at the bottom.

   You have now made up two quite complicated family trees.

3. Take one family each. Transfer the information from your cards on to the 'family trees'.

Family cards

Copy on to coloured card, one sheet for each pair. Cut out to make a pile.

Josef Oppenheimer born in 1866

Meta Oppenheimer born in 1876

Hans Felix Oppenheimer born in 1901

Rita Oppenheimer born in 1902

Paul Oppenheimer born in 1928

Corinne Oppenheimer born in 1936

Copy on to coloured card, one sheet for each pair. Cut out to make a pile.

Nicholas Oppenheimer born in 1965

Julie Oppenheimer born in 1964

Alexander Oppenheimer born in 1996

Sarah Ellen O'Connor born in 1850

William O'Connor born in 1852

James O'Connor born in 1882

THE TWENTIETH-CENTURY WORLD SUPPORT MATERIALS © JOHN MURRAY

Copy on to coloured card, one sheet for each pair. Cut out to make a pile.

Elizabeth O'Connor born 1884

Frank O'Connor born 1928

Madge O'Connor born 1926

Carmel O'Connor born 1959

Gerald Hale (married Carmel) born 1960

Michael Hale born 1986 and William Hale born 1991

The O'Connor family tree

Copy for each pair of pupils.

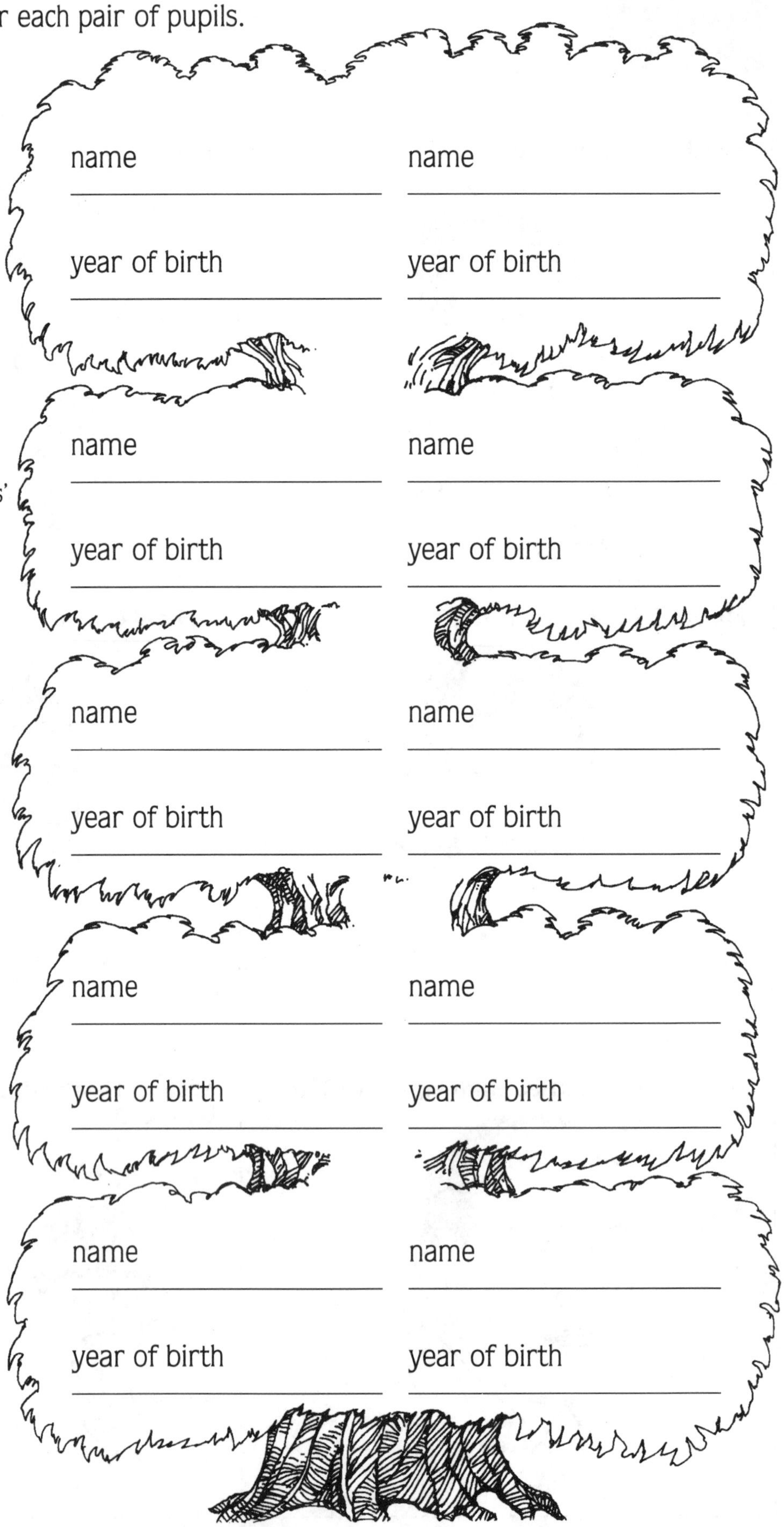

your great-great-
grandparents'
generation
1851–1880

name
_____

name
_____

year of birth
_____

year of birth
_____

your great-grandparents'
generation
1881–1910

name
_____

name
_____

year of birth
_____

year of birth
_____

your grandparents'
generation
1911–1940

name
_____

name
_____

year of birth
_____

year of birth
_____

your parents'
generation
1941–1970

name
_____

name
_____

year of birth
_____

year of birth
_____

today's
generation
1971–2000

name
_____

name
_____

year of birth
_____

year of birth
_____

The Oppenheimer family tree

Copy for each pair of pupils.

your great-great-
grandparents'
generation
1851–1880

name
_____

year of birth
_____

name
_____

year of birth
_____

your great-grandparents'
generation
1881–1910

name
_____

year of birth
_____

name
_____

year of birth
_____

your grandparents'
generation
1911–1940

name
_____

year of birth
_____

name
_____

year of birth
_____

your parents'
generation
1941–1970

name
_____

year of birth
_____

name
_____

year of birth
_____

today's
generation
1971–2000

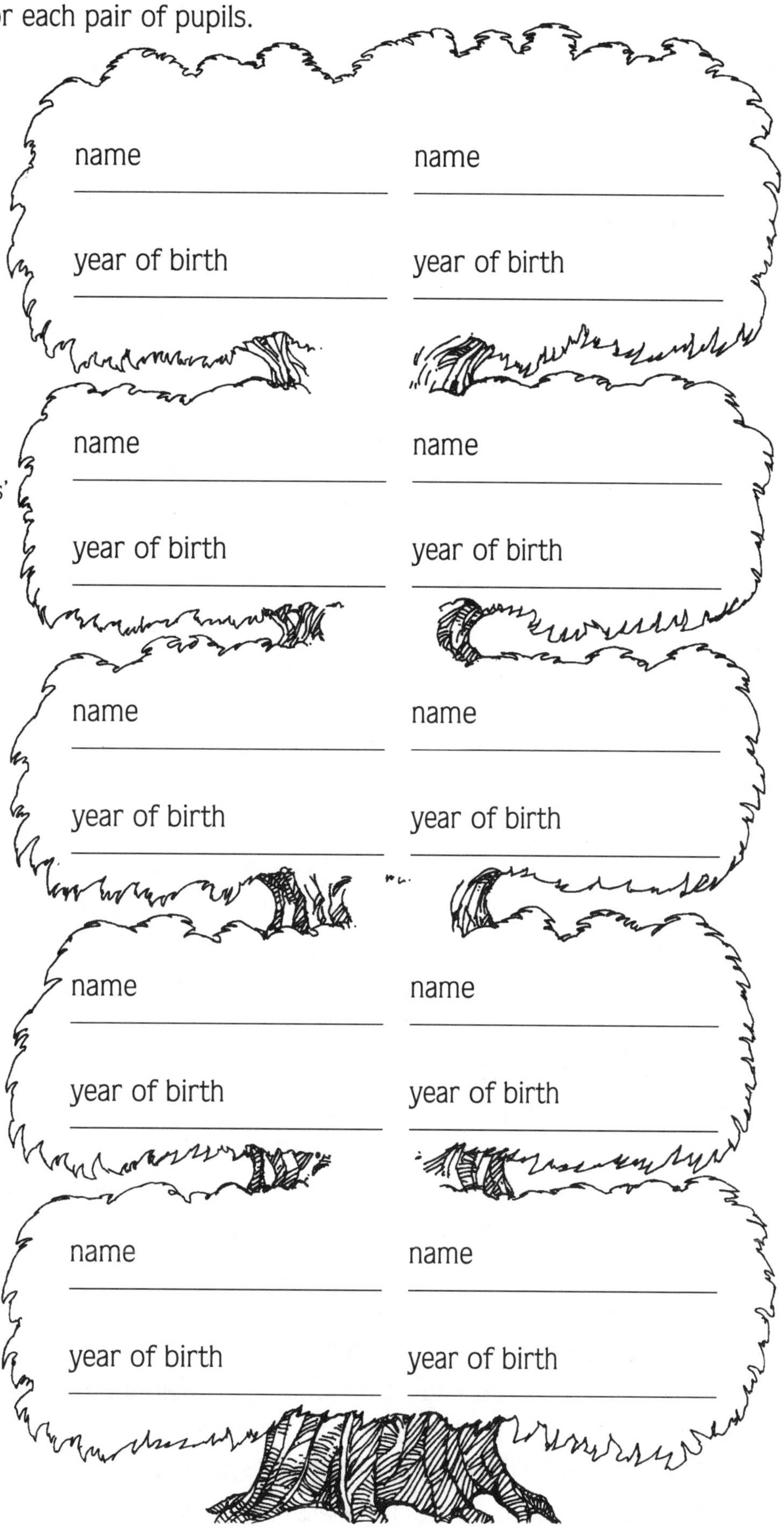

name
_____

year of birth
_____

name
_____

year of birth
_____

3

You will need

- pen or pencil

The O'Connors of Liverpool

You have now got a picture in your mind of what some of the O'Connor family looked like. Carmel O'Connor and her husband Gerry (see opposite) still live in Liverpool. In fact, they live in the same house that Carmel's parents and grandparents used to live in. Carmel's own children play in the same kitchen, sleep in the same bedrooms and eat their meals in the same dining room as their grandfather Frank O'Connor and their great-grandfather James O'Connor did.

Your task

You could work in pairs for this task.

1. Read the story about the O'Connors and the house in Jubilee Avenue where they lived at the time of the First World War.
2. Discuss with your partner anything about the O'Connors' lives and home which you think are different from nowadays. (You could underline them in the story.)
3. Record these differences in the first column of the chart on page 5.
4. When you have done this, record in the next column what it is like nowadays.
5. Finally, try to think of as many reasons as you can, why each aspect of life has changed. (The first one has been done for you.)

Story: The O'Connors of Jubilee Avenue

James and Elizabeth O'Connor were just like many other decent, hard-working couples living in Liverpool at the time of the First World War. James worked in insurance at the Royal Liver Buildings near the Pier Head. He was a clerk whose main job was to keep all the accounts in order. The accounts were written by hand into a special book called a ledger, which was locked away every night in a big, iron safe. It was a lovely building to work in. From his office James could see the ferries as they steamed across the River Mersey to Birkenhead and Wallasey.

James was given an extra job during the First World War. He had to record all the shipments that arrived at the Liverpool docks from America and parts of the British Empire. James was pleased to be able to help the war effort in this way. He could not go to fight in the War because he had bad bronchitis which he had caught when he worked in the Lancashire cotton mills as a boy. Every day after school, from the age of eight to fourteen, James had earned money by helping to clean out the cotton from under the huge machines. At that time James and his mother needed all the money they could get because James' father drank so much.

3
☞

Elizabeth stayed at home, looking after their children. Before she married James, Elizabeth had made and sold hats for a living. The drawing opposite shows Elizabeth on her wedding day.

Elizabeth and James had met when she took rooms in a boarding house in Seacombe. He was such a quiet, dignified-looking man. Elizabeth knew at once that he had suffered great hardships as a child.

Elizabeth soon discovered what those hardships were when James invited her to meet his mother Sarah Ellen. Phew, what a miserable-looking woman her future mother-in-law was. But then it all came out. Sarah Ellen had married James' father, William, when she was very young. He was an elementary schoolteacher, so, for her, it had been a good catch. Then the demon drink took hold. Within a few years William had lost his job as a teacher. He lost all his money gambling on cock fights, and then he and his family had been evicted from their home.

Sarah Ellen and her young son James found lodgings in Seacombe, but William went to the workhouse. He died soon after. Poor Sarah Ellen. She was so upset when she signed William's death certificate (below) which recorded that he had died in the Union Workhouse.

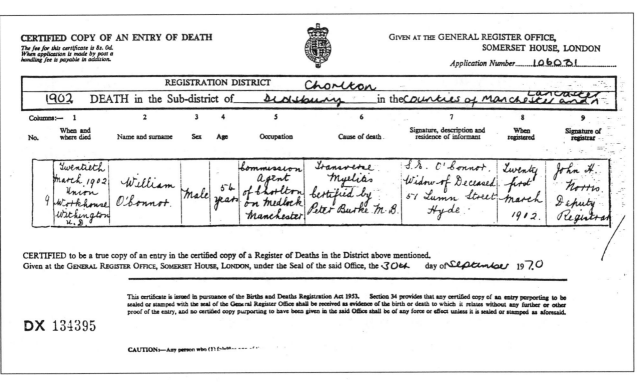

CERTIFIED COPY OF AN ENTRY OF DEATH

The fee for this certificate is 8s. 0d.
When application is made by post a handling fee is payable in addition.

GIVEN AT THE GENERAL REGISTER OFFICE, SOMERSET HOUSE, LONDON

Application Number...... 106031

	REGISTRATION DISTRICT	Chorlton	
1902	DEATH in the Sub-district of Didsbury	in the Counties of Manchester and Lancaster	

No.	When and where died	Name and surname	Sex	Age	Occupation	Cause of death	Signature, description and residence of informant	When registered	Signature of registrar
9	Twentieth March 1902 Union Workhouse Withington U.D.	William O'Connor	Male	54 years	Commission agent of Chorlton on Medlock Manchester	Transverse Myelitis certified by Peter Burke M.B.	S.E. O'Connor Widow of Deceased 51 Lumn Street Hyde	Twenty first March 1912	John H. Norris Deputy Registrar

CERTIFIED to be a true copy of an entry in the certified copy of a Register of Deaths in the District above mentioned.
Given at the GENERAL REGISTER OFFICE, SOMERSET HOUSE, LONDON, under the Seal of the said Office, the 30th day of September 1970.

This certificate is issued in pursuance of the Births and Deaths Registration Act 1953. Section 34 provides that any certified copy of an entry purporting to be sealed or stamped with the seal of the General Register Office shall be received as evidence of the birth or death to which it relates without any further or other proof of the entry, and no certified copy purporting to have been given in the said Office shall be of any force or effect unless it is sealed or stamped as aforesaid.

DX 134395

CAUTION:—Any person who (1) falsifies any of...

3 ☞

All of that sad history was in the past now. James and Elizabeth got married in 1909. Five of their eight children were born within a few years of each other. Molly was the oldest. She was born in 1910, the year that Edward VII had died and George V became King. Kay was born in 1916. James was very fond of the family photograph which had been taken soon after Kay was born. It had pride of place on his desk at work.

There was Sarah Ellen with her usual grim face, but the rest of the family looked lovely. James, his eldest son, stood next to his big sister Molly. Then there was Winifred who was only eighteen months old, sitting on her father's knee. Next came Louis, a strange name for a boy, but Sarah Ellen had insisted. 'My family escaped to England during the French Revolution. It has royal blood in its veins,' she said. 'My grandson will be named after one of the great kings of France, Louis XIV (14), the Sun King!' Nobody knew where the story had come from but Sarah Ellen got her own way! Finally, the new baby Kay was on her mother's knee.

Every day James thanked his lucky stars that his children were too young to take part in the War that was raging across Europe. Maisie, the O'Connors' domestic servant, had not been so lucky. Her eldest brother and her fiancé were killed early in 1915, whilst poor Mr Yates who lived across the road had lost both sons at the Battle of the Somme in August 1916.

James was lucky. He had a decent salary of £250 a year. This meant he was able to buy his own house and invite his mother Sarah Ellen to come and live with them. The house he bought was a roomy, Victorian, semi-detached house near Broadgreen railway station. It was a famous railway line. The children were often told how their great-uncle Albert had been a navvy, building the line from Liverpool to Rainhill in 1830. Broadgreen was certainly a convenient place to live. James had only a two-minute walk to catch the steam train into Liverpool Lime Street to get to work. From there it was a short tram ride to the Royal Liver Buildings.

THE TWENTIETH-CENTURY WORLD SUPPORT MATERIALS © JOHN MURRAY

〰〰〰〰〰〰〰〰〰〰〰〰〰〰〰〰〰〰〰

The O'Connors' house had four large bedrooms, two rooms in the attic, a sitting room, a dining room, a morning room and a kitchen. (You can see what the outside of the house looked like from the drawing opposite.) The washhouse and coal-shed were right next to the morning room. This meant that Maisie, the O'Connors' servant, didn't have far to carry all the heavy, wet washing from the dolly tub to the mangle, and then back into the house to hang up in the kitchen.

Maisie Morgan always told people how fortunate she was to be working for such a nice couple. She had her own bedroom in the attic. It was quite large for a servant's room but it was cold in winter because there was no fireplace. Maisie didn't mind this too much seeing as she spent most of her time in the kitchen or the washhouse where the heat from the stove or the dolly tub kept her warm enough! (You can see Maisie using the dolly tub in this drawing.) She didn't have far to fetch the coal either, which was just as well because Sarah Ellen expected to see a coal fire burning in all the downstairs rooms when she got up every morning.

Changes in our way of life over the twentieth century

Use the chart below to complete the task on page 1.

What life was like at the time of the First World War	What life is like now	Reasons why it has changed
James wrote all his accounts in a ledger.	People use calculators and store information on computers.	■ Electric adding machines were invented, then huge computers, then microchips. Now we have computers that can do almost anything. ■ More people needed insurance so James' way of doing things was too slow.

THE TWENTIETH-CENTURY WORLD SUPPORT MATERIALS © JOHN MURRAY

〰〰〰〰〰〰〰〰〰〰〰〰〰〰〰〰〰〰〰〰〰〰〰〰〰〰

♦ **HISTORY DICTIONARY**

The important words	My explanation of them
Edwardian	_____

Your task 📑

The beginning of the twentieth century is often called the Edwardian Era because King Edward ruled the country at that time. Below are some household objects which would have been in many **Edwardian** houses. Match the right name to each picture.

- ▪ basin & ewer
- ▪ gas lamp
- ▪ dolly stick
- ▪ aspidistra
- ▪ coal scuttle
- ▪ piano
- ▪ mangle
- ▪ carpet beater
- ▪ fire screen
- ▪ linen press
- ▪ occasional table
- ▪ iron

Your task

Some of the objects on the previous page are still with us in the 1990s. Some have disappeared. Some have changed a great deal. Some are used as ornaments in houses where people want to recreate an 'Edwardian style'.

1. Make a list of those objects which are still used today.

2. Make a list of those objects which have changed or disappeared or are just used as ornaments. Next to each object, write down what you think has taken its place, e.g. the carpet beater has been replaced by the vacuum cleaner.

Objects which are still used today

_____

_____

_____

_____

_____

_____

Objects which are no longer used

carpet beater _____

_____

_____

_____

_____

_____

Objects which have replaced them

vacuum cleaner _____

_____

_____

_____

_____

_____

4

You will need
- pen or pencil

Shopping: then and now

Although Molly O'Connor was only seven years old, it was her job to take the shopping lists to the local shops. There, the shopkeeper would pack a big box full of the things that the family needed. James would then collect the boxes on his way home from work.

Every week, Molly and her grandma Sarah Ellen would check what was in the kitchen and pantry. Then Grandma would sit down with Molly and help her to write out the weekly shopping list. Sarah Ellen wrote down the price of each item so that Molly would be able to give the shopkeeper the correct amount of money. You can see the list on page 2.

Your task

(Molly's grandma would have used old money – pounds, shillings and pence. For this task, the prices are written as they would have been in new money. This will help you to compare the difference between how much things cost then and how much they cost now.)

1. Read each item on Molly's list.
2. Find the corresponding item on the 1990s supermarket list on page 3. Record what the item would cost now in the space provided.
3. Add up the totals for each list.

☞ **Molly's shopping list**

In the final column, write what each item would cost now. Add up the two totals.

Type of shop	Name of item	Cost then	Cost now
baker	large loaf	5p	
butcher	3 lb beef	9p	
the dairy	1 lb butter	6p	
grocer	packet of tea	4p	
costermonger	2 lb apples	4p	
greengrocer	5 lb potatoes	3p	
haberdasher	packet of needles	2p	
grocer	jar of Bovril	2p	
butcher	1 lb lard	3p	
grocer	1 lb currants	3p	
grocer	5 lb sugar	5p	
grocer	tin of mustard	1p	
ironmongers	slab of soap	2p	
grocer	salt	1p	
fishmonger	fish	2p	
butcher	2 lb bacon	6p	
haberdasher	yellow ribbons	1p	
grocer	3 lb flour	3p	
butcher	rabbit	3p	
the dairy	dozen eggs	5p	
grocer	jelly crystals	3p	
	Total		

4

Supermarket list from the 1990s

Use the 1990s shopping list below to fill in the final column of Molly's shopping list on page 2.

- **Which were the most expensive items during the First World War?**
- **Which items appear on Molly's shopping list that would NOT appear on YOUR family's list?**

Your task

You could work in pairs for this task.

1. On page 4 make a list of all the different types of groceries that YOU think would NOT have been around when Molly was writing HER shopping list. A few examples have been given to help get you started.

2. When you have completed your list:
   - compare it with other people's lists
   - check with your teacher that the food you have mentioned really DIDN'T exist 80 years ago.

1 lb butter	£1.80
1 lb currants	60p
1 lb lard	80p
2 lb apples	90p
2 lb bacon	£6.00
3 lb beef	£10.00
5 lb potatoes	£1.50
5 lb sugar	£1.80
dozen eggs	£1.60
fish (mackerel)	£2.00
flour 3 lb	75p
jar of Bovril	£2.29
jelly crystals	89p
large loaf	50p
packet of needles	£1.49
packet of tea	80p
rabbit	£6.50
salt	49p
slab of soap	80p
tin of mustard	£1.39
yellow ribbons	30p

 What else is different about shopping then from shopping now?

Groceries which would not have been on Molly's shopping list

Names _____ & _____

Instant Whip

Sour cream & chives Tortilla Chips

Honey nut loops

5

The Oppenheimers of Nuremberg in Germany

At the beginning of the First World War, Hans Oppenheimer was only thirteen years old. Hans lived with his parents, Josef and Meta, in a large detached house in one of the best areas of Nuremberg.

Hans' father Josef was a textile merchant. He must have been extremely good at his job to be able to afford such a big house. Josef's wife Meta was the daughter of a doctor. Both of them were Jewish. Their families had lived in Germany for more than a century. The Oppenheimer family was proud to be Jewish but, just like many Christian families or families from other faiths, they did not consider their religion to be something that separated them from their friends and neighbours.

Hans had an older brother called Rudi and a younger sister called Liesl. They were much more outgoing and fun-loving than Hans. He was the quiet one whilst the other two were always fooling around and 'acting like kids' as Hans would remind them! You can see Rudi and Liesl in the drawing below.

Hans and his parents are dead now, but we can imagine what living in this smart area of Nuremberg was like. The house was enormous. Parts of it dated back to the sixteenth century, so there were tall chimneys and windows with leaded panes. Other parts had been added or changed during the nineteenth century and the walls were covered with cream-coloured plaster. It was a wonderful place to grow up.

With such a big house, the Oppenheimers needed several servants. Before the War there would have have been a nanny for the children, a cook, two maids, a butler and at least two gardeners. During the War, most of the domestic servants would have 'joined up'. The men went to fight at the Front against the British. The women would have gone to work in the big 'arms' factories just outside Nuremberg.

During the War Rudi, Hans and Liesl still went to school. Their parents were at home. Their mother Meta was a good cook, so they managed very well, especially as they could grow so many things in their garden.

Hans studied hard at school. He loved to read about the famous German philosophers and psychologists who had been alive in the previous century. They had made such an important contribution to German society and many of them were Jewish. It made Hans proud to be German and to be Jewish as well. He knew that people were suffering because of the War. Like millions of other Germans, he was determined that when he grew up, he would do everything he could to make sure that there would never be another war.

Your task

You only have fifteen minutes to complete this task!
You should work in pairs. You will need to be able to refer back to the work you did on the O'Connor family.

It is February 1917. Hans' mother Meta is trying to keep everybody's spirits up. She has found her old sketch pad. Inside are drawings that she did when the children were small.

Look carefully at Meta's drawings on page 3. List all the clues from these drawings and from the information about both families which show that the Oppenheimers were wealthier than the O'Connors.

👉

My two little boys Rudi and Hans with their nanny. It won't be long before Hans starts wearing his sailor suit too.

Meta Oppenheimer
1910
Liesl in her best hat

Meta Oppenheimer
July 1904.

Meta Oppenheimer
1905
Our footman Rudi is very unkind! He calls him Mr Grumpy.

5

Clues which tell us that the Oppenheimer family was much wealthier than the O'Connor family

DEPTH STUDY 1
The First World War

♦ **HISTORY DICTIONARY**

The important words	My explanation of them
long-term causes	_____
	_____
short-term causes	_____
	_____
alliance	_____
the Great War	_____

In this depth study you will find out what caused the First World War, and what life was like for the soldiers who fought in it.

■ You will discover that there were many reasons why the War began. Some were **long-term causes** of the War. (They had been developing for a long time.) Some were **short-term causes**. (They were events which helped trigger the start of the War.)

■ You will find out about the **alliances** which helped cause the War. France, Russia and Great Britain were in one alliance. Germany, Austria–Hungary and Italy were in another.

■ You will find out how long the War lasted, who won, and how many people died.

■ You will discover who fought in the War and what life was like for soldiers in the trenches.

We now call this war the First World War but people at that time called it the 'Great War'. It is where the symbol of the red poppy comes from. Poppies grew in the fields where most of the fighting took place. It is in those fields that millions of men died. The War ended on 11 November 1918, so this is the date when the men who died are remembered. Many people buy poppies. They wear them as a sign of respect for all those people who have died in wars.

6

You will need
• pen or pencil

Why were Germany and Britain getting ready for war?

Many historians think that Germany and Britain were getting ready for War because each country was suspicious, greedy and wanted more money and power. They also think that Germany and Britain wanted to try out their new ships and war weapons. Other historians say that the countries of Europe had hated each other for centuries. They remind us that they had been going to war with each other, on and off, ever since the Roman Empire collapsed in the fifth century! They say that these countries would look for any excuse to start a war.

As usual, when you are studying history, no one is completely right and no one is completely wrong. There were several reasons why the First World War began.

Your task

Read this story. It was written to try and explain to young children some of the reasons why the First World War began. The story concentrates on telling children about Britain and Germany. Remember, it was written in a very simple way and from a British viewpoint.

As you read this story, underline in blue the sentences which tell you why Britain might want a war with Germany. Underline in red the sentences which tell you why Germany might want a war with Britain. Then complete the chart on page 3.

Story: Two suspicious countries

George V, the British King, was the cousin of Kaiser (Emperor) Wilhelm of Germany. The two men pretended to be friends. However, they were very suspicious of each other.

The people of Great Britain did not like the Germans. In 1909, an article in the *Daily Mail* said:

'Germany is deliberately preparing to destroy the British Empire . . . Britain alone stands in the way of Germany's path to world power and domination.'

King George and his advisers were jealous of Kaiser Wilhelm because Germany was a successful country. It was getting richer and stronger all the time. It was bigger than Britain. Germany had more soldiers than Britain. Britain worried that Germany was getting too strong. So they made an alliance with France and Russia, who were Germany's neighbours.

The Kaiser and his advisers were jealous of Britain because Britain's empire was bigger. Britain also had more ships and submarines. They were worried about Britain making an alliance with France and Russia. They felt surrounded by enemies who might attack them. So they made their own alliance with Austria–Hungary and Italy. They also made a secret plan called the Schlieffen Plan. Their plan was to beat their enemies one by one. They would attack France first. Once France was defeated, they would attack Russia.

For a while, King George and Kaiser Wilhelm were very polite to each other. Their prime ministers and foreign ministers visited each other's countries. But in secret each country was spying on the other. Each country was building more warships and trying out new weapons.

Britain and Germany were both waiting for an excuse to go to war with each other. In 1914 they got it.

Complete the chart below when you have read the story of two suspicious countries.

Reasons why Britain might want a war with Germany	Reasons why Germany might want a war with Britain

THE TWENTIETH-CENTURY WORLD SUPPORT MATERIALS © JOHN MURRAY

7

There are three pages to this task

~~~~~~

You will need

- coloured pens or pencils
- a calculator

Which alliance was stronger?

Germany's alliance was called the Triple Alliance. There were three countries in the alliance – Germany, Italy and Austria–Hungary. When they pooled their resources together, they were very strong as you can see from the chart below.

Your task

1. Count up the Triple Alliance's total strength (population has already been done for you).

The Triple Alliance

	Germany	Italy	Austria–Hungary	Total
population	65 million	35 million	50 million	150 million
soldiers	2,200,000 (two million two hundred thousand)	750,000 (seven hundred and fifty thousand)	810,000 (eight hundred and ten thousand)	
ships and submarines	110	48	90	
money spent on weapons	£60,000,000 (sixty million)	£10,000,000 (ten million)	£22,000,000 (twenty-two million)	
people in their empire	15,000,000 (fifteen million)	2,000,000 (two million)	0 (none)	

Britain's alliance was called the Triple Entente. There were also three countries in it – Britain, France and Russia. These three countries were very strong too when they joined together.

2. Count up the Triple Entente's total strength (population has already been done for you).

The Triple Entente

	Britain	France	Russia	Total
population	45,000,000 (forty-five million)	40,000,000 (forty million)	64,000,000 (sixty-four million)	149,000,000 (one hundred and forty-nine million)
soldiers	711,000 (seven hundred and eleven thousand)	1,250,000 (one million two hundred and fifty thousand)	1,200,000 (one million two hundred thousand)	
ships and submarines	249	35	39	
money spent on weapons	£50,000,000 (fifty million)	£37,000,000 (thirty-seven million)	£67,000,000 (sixty-seven million)	
people in their empire	390,000,000 (three hundred and ninety million)	58,000,000 (fifty-eight million)	0 (none)	

© JOHN MURRAY   *THE TWENTIETH-CENTURY WORLD SUPPORT MATERIALS*

53

3. Use the information from the two grids to complete the chart below.

Total strength	Triple Alliance Germany, Italy, Austria–Hungary	Triple Entente Britain, France, Russia
population (number of people in the country)		
soldiers		
ships and submarines		
money spent on weapons		
people in their empire		

Your task

Now examine each of the six individual countries.

1. Which country do you think was the strongest in 1914? Explain your answer carefully.

_____

_____

_____

2. Which ALLIANCE or group of countries do you think was the stronger? Explain your answer carefully.

_____

_____

_____

3. Now try to answer this question: Did King George V and Kaiser Wilhelm have any real reason to be jealous of each other?

_____

_____

_____

Your task 🔍 📝 ✏️

Examine the map below. It shows Europe in 1914. It shows you where the six countries are. But it only gives you their initials.

1. Use the information you already have to complete the names of each country.
2. Decide whether they belong to the Triple Alliance or the Triple Entente.
3. Shade the Triple Alliance countries in one colour and the Triple Entente countries in another.
4. Add your colour key to the map.

> 💬 ■ **Look carefully at the map you have just completed.**
> ■ **Do you think that the countries of the Triple Alliance and the Triple Entente were right to be suspicious of each other?**

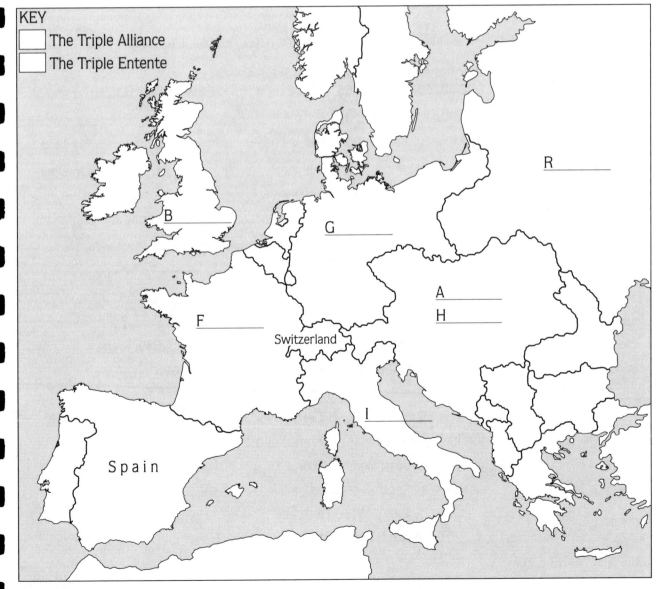

KEY
☐ The Triple Alliance
☐ The Triple Entente

Europe in 1914

8

You will need

• pen or pencil

What events triggered the First World War?

Britain was suspicious of Germany, Austria–Hungary was suspicious of Russia, France was suspicious of Italy, and so on. Some of these suspicions had gone on for hundreds of years.

Some suspicions were quite recent. For instance, Britain and Germany had only been arguing about their empires for 40 years. The race to be the strongest country with the most ships, submarines and war weapons had really only begun in the early 1900s.

All these suspicions made Europe a tense place.

Most historians agree that by 1914 Britain and Germany were looking for an excuse to start a war and settle things once and for all. No one expected a long war. They just wanted a short war which would show who was strongest. On 28 June 1914, they found their excuse. It happened in a place called Sarajevo, in Bosnia, then part of Austria–Hungary.

Your task

Here are the events of nine different days in the months before the beginning of the War. They have been muddled up.

On pages 2–3 are nine cartoon pictures. These are in the correct order.

Write the correct explanation underneath each cartoon.

1 August: Germany declared war on Russia. It also began to move its army towards France and Belgium.	28 July: Austria–Hungary declared war on Serbia. Belgrade, the capital of Serbia, was attacked.	2 August: The French army was put on war alert, ready to fight any German invasion.
6 August: To complete the picture, Austria–Hungary declared war on Russia.	28 June: The heir to the Austrian throne, Archduke Franz Ferdinand, was killed in Sarajevo by a Bosnian Serb.	23 July: Austria–Hungary blamed Serbia for the death of Archduke Franz Ferdinand.
30 July: Germany sent a message to Russia ordering it not to help Serbia.	3 and 4 August: Germany declared war on France and invaded Belgium. Britain ordered Germany to leave Belgium. When Germany refused, Britain declared war.	29 July: The Russian army got ready to help Serbia defend itself against the Austrian attack.

8 ☞

Steps to war

28 June
The heir to the Austrian throne, Archduke Franz Ferdinand, is assassinated in Bosnia

The Russian army gets ready to help Serbia defend itself against the Austrian attack

To complete the picture Austria declares war on Russia

FRANCE
BRITAIN
RUSSIA

Germany sends a demand to Russia ordering it to hold back from helping Serbia

Austria declares war on Serbia. Belgrade (in Serbia) is shelled

Now complete this sentence.

By 6 August 1914 two members of the Triple Alliance, _____ and

_____ , were at war with all three members of the Triple Entente,

_____ , _____ and _____ .

The First World War had begun.

9

You will need

- pen or pencil

What were the causes of the First World War?

Your task

You are now ready to write an essay about the First World War. The title of the essay is:

What were the causes of the First World War?

Planning the essay

Where will I get the correct information?

You have already done a great deal of preparation for this essay. All the information you need will be on your worksheets or in your textbooks or folders.

How can I sort all this information out?

1. Read through all your work.
2. Make a list of all causes of the First World War that you have found out about.
3. Organise them under two headings:

a) long-term causes

_____

_____

_____

_____

b) short-term causes or triggers

_____

_____

_____

_____

~~~~~~

4. Now decide which were the most important causes and number them in order of importance. Start with No. 1 – the most important. No. 2 is the second most important and so on.

How do I turn this information into an essay?

If you follow the plan below, you will be able to write a very good essay.

paragraph 1   Make this a short **introduction** explaining that there were many causes of the First World War, but that some are more important than others.

paragraph 2   This is where you make a note of all the **long-term causes** of the War.

paragraph 3   This is where you make a note of the **short-term causes or triggers** of the War.

paragraph 4   In your conclusion, decide which YOU think were the **most important causes**. Note these down. Explain why you think they were the most important causes.

Some more helpful hints

You are using each piece of **information to give evidence** in your essay about what caused the First World War to begin. Obviously this means you must keep mentioning the word **cause**! Think about using sentences like 'One important cause of the First World War was . . .' or 'Even though it had gone on for hundreds of years, another important cause was . . .' or 'Probably the most important cause was . . .'

Now write your essay on the sheet provided on page 3.

Name _____ Form _____ Date _____

What were the causes of the First World War?

_____

_____

_____

_____

_____

_____

_____

_____

_____

_____

_____

_____

_____

_____

_____

10

What was trench warfare?

You will need

- coloured pens or pencils
- tracing paper
- A4 paper

◆ **HISTORY DICTIONARY**

The important words	My explanation of them
trench warfare	_____
	_____

When the War began on 4 August 1914, both sides thought that it would be over by Christmas. They thought that their superior armies would quickly attack and defeat the enemy. But it didn't happen like this. Instead, the two armies got stuck halfway across Europe. Each side dug huge trenches into the ground so that the soldiers would have somewhere to hide when they weren't fighting.

These trenches were two metres deep and stretched from Belgium right through to Switzerland. The British dug one set of trenches to try to protect French and British soldiers. A few hundred metres away, the Germans dug another set to try to protect German and Austrian soldiers.

Soldiers crept out at night to run across and attack the other side's trenches. The space in between the German and British trenches was called 'no man's land', probably because no man with any sense would go into it of his own accord! Both sides fired machine-guns and shells at their enemy's trenches. We call this kind of fighting **trench warfare**.

The trenches were probably the most dangerous, frightening, dirty and unhealthy places in the world! This drawing shows you what the inside of a trench would have looked like.

THE TWENTIETH-CENTURY WORLD SUPPORT MATERIALS © JOHN MURRAY

The Western Front: 1914–1918

Your task

This map shows you where the trenches (or the Western Front as it was called) were dug.

1. Shade the trenches in brown and outline them with black barbed wire.
2. Find Luxembourg. Colour it yellow.
3. Find Holland. Colour it orange.
4. Find the left-hand side of Germany. Colour it green.
5. Find Belgium. Colour it red.
6. Find France. Colour it blue.

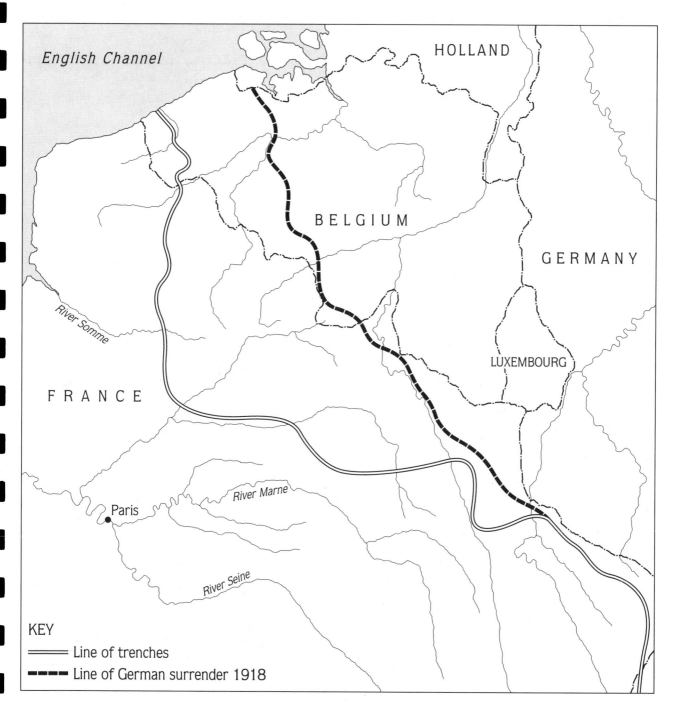

KEY

===== Line of trenches

▄▄▄▄ Line of German surrender 1918

Your task A

Read these verses from a poem written by John McCrae who was a doctor in the First World War. Answer the questions below.

In Flanders field the poppies blow
Between the crosses, row on row,
That mark our place; and in the sky
The larks, still bravely singing, fly
Scarce heard amidst the guns below.

We are the Dead. Short days ago
We lived, felt dawn, saw sunset glow,
Loved and were loved, and now we lie
In Flanders fields.

1. What was the name of the place of Europe where most of the fighting took place?

_____

2. Whose places do you think the crosses were marking?

_____

3. What do you think 'Loved and were loved' means?

_____

_____

Your task B

The author of the poem, John McCrae, has asked you to illustrate these two verses for him. He wants everyone to understand the message of the poem.

   Use a sheet of A4 paper.

■ You could trace some of these designs to use as templates.

■ You could read the whole of his poem to find out what else he said.

■ You could look at war paintings and photographs to help you with your design.

11

Who fought in the trenches?

Virtually every single family in the British Empire lost a loved one in the War.

The British army had English, Scottish, Irish, Welsh, Asian, African, Caribbean, Canadian and Australian men fighting for it. It didn't matter what race or colour a soldier was. It didn't matter whether a soldier was rich or poor. When they were sent to serve on the Western Front their chance of survival was very small.

Your task

Here are pictures drawn by a British soldier, A.D. Langhorne, who was serving in the trenches. He wrote a description on the back of each picture.

1. Match the descriptions below to the correct pictures.
2. Write the correct description underneath each picture.

- ■ **a soldier from the British West Indies**
- ■ **British Staff Officer**
- ■ **Indian Cavalry Division, Bengal Lancers**
- ■ **Australasian soldier**

- ■ **How many pupils in the class have great-grandparents or great-uncles who fought in the First World War?**
- ■ **How are they remembered by the rest of the family?**

12

You will need

- a dice
- counters

Telegrams from the trenches: an activity

It is August 1914. You are a young soldier who has joined up and been sent to the Western Front. Will you return safely or will your family get a telegram announcing your death?

Your task

You should be in groups of three or four to play the game on pages 3–4.

1. Start the game in August 1914.
2. Take it in turns to throw the dice.
3. Every time you land on a square, read out what has happened to you to the rest of your group, then record the date on one of the Diary Record cards on page 5.
4. If you are killed, you must record the date on your Diary Record card. Collect a new card, give yourself a new name, and rejoin the game at the beginning of the next year.
5. The game continues for about fifteen minutes OR until the first person makes it to November 1918.

At the end of the game, discuss the questions below.

- How many soldiers (people in the class) were killed? (i.e. how many Diary Record cards were completed!)
- What do you think were the worst things that could happen to you in the trenches?
- What events would have caused you the most despair and unhappiness?

12

Your task

1. Take a copy of the game. Choose one of your Diary Record cards where you recorded the dates of the squares you landed on.
Use your Regimental Diary sheet on page 6.
Give yourself a name.
In the space next to each date, use the information from the squares you landed on to write, **in your own words**, what happened to you and how you felt.

2. It is 50 years since the end of the First World War. Your grandchildren ask you what life was like in the trenches. Use the sheet on page 7, 'My life in the trenches', to write down what you would tell them.

You could

- use the information from your diary
- use the knowledge you have from the poems and other information you have been given.

You could write about

- when you were 'called up'
- what the trenches looked like
- what the soldiers wore
- what you ate
- what it was like when you crept into no man's land
- what happened when a soldier was killed
- what happened when a soldier deserted.

You could finish by talking about your own personal feelings at having survived this terrible war.

Gameboard: life in the trenches

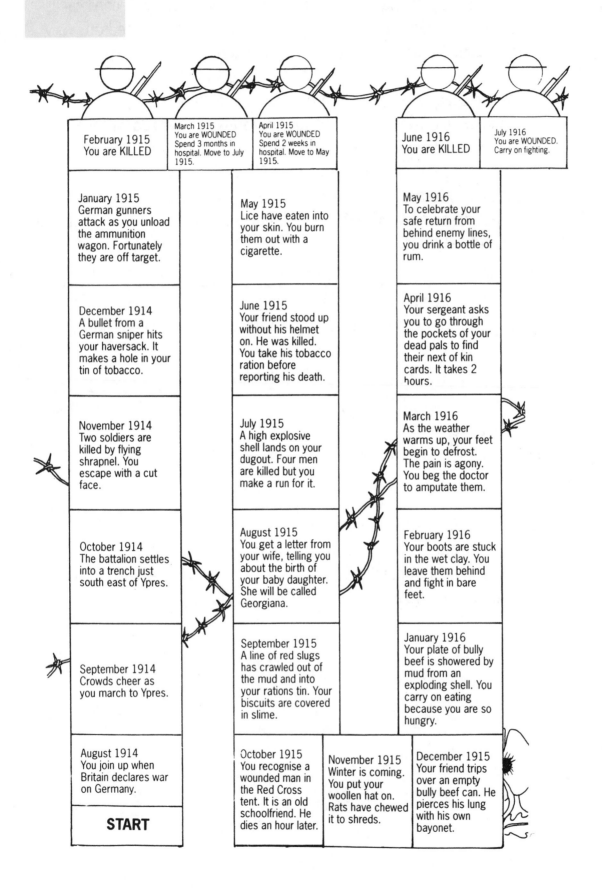

| February 1915 You are KILLED | March 1915 You are WOUNDED Spend 3 months in hospital. Move to July 1915. | April 1915 You are WOUNDED Spend 2 weeks in hospital. Move to May 1915. | | June 1916 You are KILLED | July 1916 You are WOUNDED. Carry on fighting. |

January 1915
German gunners attack as you unload the ammunition wagon. Fortunately they are off target.

May 1915
Lice have eaten into your skin. You burn them out with a cigarette.

May 1916
To celebrate your safe return from behind enemy lines, you drink a bottle of rum.

December 1914
A bullet from a German sniper hits your haversack. It makes a hole in your tin of tobacco.

June 1915
Your friend stood up without his helmet on. He was killed. You take his tobacco ration before reporting his death.

April 1916
Your sergeant asks you to go through the pockets of your dead pals to find their next of kin cards. It takes 2 hours.

November 1914
Two soldiers are killed by flying shrapnel. You escape with a cut face.

July 1915
A high explosive shell lands on your dugout. Four men are killed but you make a run for it.

March 1916
As the weather warms up, your feet begin to defrost. The pain is agony. You beg the doctor to amputate them.

October 1914
The battalion settles into a trench just south east of Ypres.

August 1915
You get a letter from your wife, telling you about the birth of your baby daughter. She will be called Georgiana.

February 1916
Your boots are stuck in the wet clay. You leave them behind and fight in bare feet.

September 1914
Crowds cheer as you march to Ypres.

September 1915
A line of red slugs has crawled out of the mud and into your rations tin. Your biscuits are covered in slime.

January 1916
Your plate of bully beef is showered by mud from an exploding shell. You carry on eating because you are so hungry.

August 1914
You join up when Britain declares war on Germany.

START

October 1915
You recognise a wounded man in the Red Cross tent. It is an old schoolfriend. He dies an hour later.

November 1915
Winter is coming. You put your woollen hat on. Rats have chewed it to shreds.

December 1915
Your friend trips over an empty bully beef can. He pierces his lung with his own bayonet.

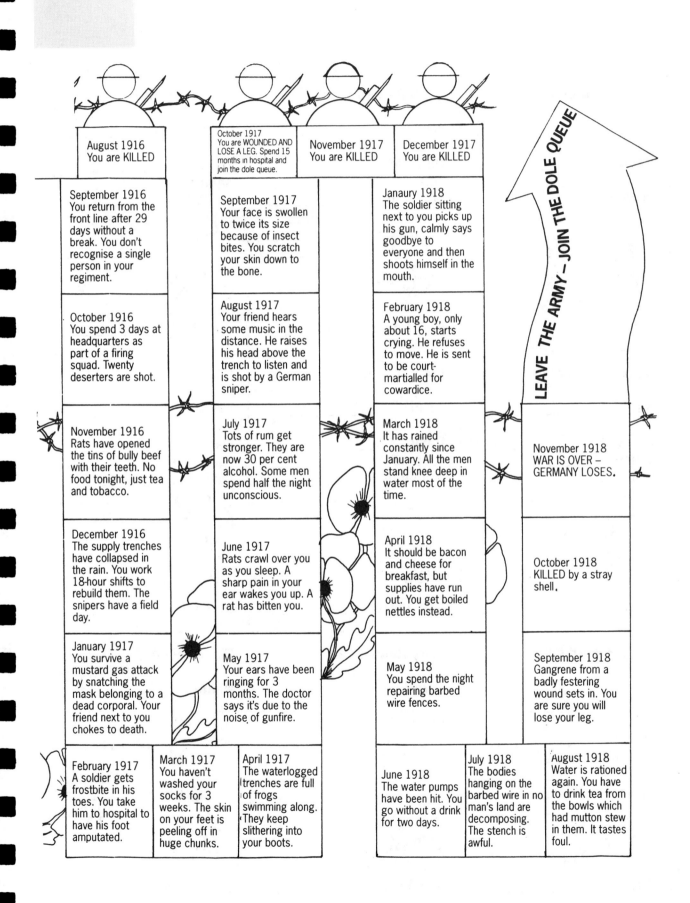

August 1916
You are KILLED

October 1917
You are WOUNDED AND LOSE A LEG. Spend 15 months in hospital and join the dole queue.

November 1917
You are KILLED

December 1917
You are KILLED

LEAVE THE ARMY – JOIN THE DOLE QUEUE

September 1916
You return from the front line after 29 days without a break. You don't recognise a single person in your regiment.

September 1917
Your face is swollen to twice its size because of insect bites. You scratch your skin down to the bone.

January 1918
The soldier sitting next to you picks up his gun, calmly says goodbye to everyone and then shoots himself in the mouth.

October 1916
You spend 3 days at headquarters as part of a firing squad. Twenty deserters are shot.

August 1917
Your friend hears some music in the distance. He raises his head above the trench to listen and is shot by a German sniper.

February 1918
A young boy, only about 16, starts crying. He refuses to move. He is sent to be court-martialled for cowardice.

November 1916
Rats have opened the tins of bully beef with their teeth. No food tonight, just tea and tobacco.

July 1917
Tots of rum get stronger. They are now 30 per cent alcohol. Some men spend half the night unconscious.

March 1918
It has rained constantly since January. All the men stand knee deep in water most of the time.

November 1918
WAR IS OVER – GERMANY LOSES.

December 1916
The supply trenches have collapsed in the rain. You work 18-hour shifts to rebuild them. The snipers have a field day.

June 1917
Rats crawl over you as you sleep. A sharp pain in your ear wakes you up. A rat has bitten you.

April 1918
It should be bacon and cheese for breakfast, but supplies have run out. You get boiled nettles instead.

October 1918
KILLED by a stray shell.

January 1917
You survive a mustard gas attack by snatching the mask belonging to a dead corporal. Your friend next to you chokes to death.

May 1917
Your ears have been ringing for 3 months. The doctor says it's due to the noise of gunfire.

May 1918
You spend the night repairing barbed wire fences.

September 1918
Gangrene from a badly festering wound sets in. You are sure you will lose your leg.

February 1917
A soldier gets frostbite in his toes. You take him to hospital to have his foot amputated.

March 1917
You haven't washed your socks for 3 weeks. The skin on your feet is peeling off in huge chunks.

April 1917
The waterlogged trenches are full of frogs swimming along. They keep slithering into your boots.

June 1918
The water pumps have been hit. You go without a drink for two days.

July 1918
The bodies hanging on the barbed wire in no man's land are decomposing. The stench is awful.

August 1918
Water is rationed again. You have to drink tea from the bowls which had mutton stew in them. It tastes foul.

Diary Record cards

Diary Record card	Diary Record card	Diary Record card
Name _____	Name _____	Name _____
Dates of squares I landed on _____	Dates of squares I landed on _____	Dates of squares I landed on _____
Date I died _____	Date I died _____	Date I died _____
Diary Record card	Diary Record card	Diary Record card
Name _____	Name _____	Name _____
Dates of squares I landed on _____	Dates of squares I landed on _____	Dates of squares I landed on _____
Date I died _____	Date I died _____	Date I died _____
Diary Record card	Diary Record card	Diary Record card
Name _____	Name _____	Name _____
Dates of squares I landed on _____	Dates of squares I landed on _____	Dates of squares I landed on _____
Date I died _____	Date I died _____	Date I died _____

THE TWENTIETH-CENTURY WORLD SUPPORT MATERIALS © JOHN MURRAY

REGIMENTAL DIARY

Property of _____

Date	Personal Record

12 👉

MY LIFE
IN THE TRENCHES

13

A comic-strip war

You will need

- coloured pens or pencils

Your task

You should work in pairs for this task.

Read the comic-strip version of life in the trenches on page 2. It is an interpretation of history. It is part of a comic which was written in 1992 – more than 70 years after the First World War ended.

1. As you read it, colour in those speech bubbles or pieces of writing which **both of you agree** tell you about things that probably DID happen in the trenches.

2. Read the three sources on page 3. They were written by people who fought in the trenches. Underline all the phrases and sentences which, **in both your opinions**, show that the **soldiers knew that they were likely to die**.

- ■ **How useful was the comic strip as a source of information about life in the trenches?**
- ■ **Was it as useful as the primary written sources?**

3. Which, **in both your opinions**, was the most useful source of evidence to an historian:

   ■ the comic-strip interpretation of history; or

   ■ the sources written by people who were there at the time?

   Explain your answer carefully.

_____

_____

_____

_____

_____

_____

_____

THE TWENTIETH-CENTURY WORLD SUPPORT MATERIALS © JOHN MURRAY

SOURCE 1 The last letter from Private Peter MacGregor to his wife in September 1916. He was killed shortly afterwards by a direct hit on his trench by an enemy shell

I am well and looking forward to the end of the War. I wish it would hurry up.

One of our men was caught by a sniper – he was standing at the entrance to his dugout, the bullet went in under his shoulder – alas, alas.

When I was standing at the cookhouse door, I saw the stretcher which came along to take the poor fellow away – how sad it was, he was carried out, wrapped up in his waterproof sheet, placed in this thing and whisked away.

The business of the hour has to go on. A dead man is no use to the army, get him out of the way as quickly as possible. War is a terrible thing and so few people realise it.

SOURCE 2 Written by a photographer, Geoffrey Malins, who was sent to France by the government to photograph the Battle of the Somme. He is describing the night before the start of the Battle of the Somme

Crowds of men were crouching round, heating up their canteens of water, some frying pieces of meat, others heating soup, and all the time laughing and talking. From other groups came the quiet humming of favourite songs . . . And these men knew they were going over the top in the morning. They knew that many would not be alive tomorrow night, yet I never saw a sad face, nor heard a word of complaint . . .

SOURCE 3 Written by Private Henry Russell about the Battle of the Somme in 1916

During our advance, I saw many of my colleagues killed by German machine gun fire.

I came to the conclusion that going on would be suicidal and that the best thing we could do would be to stay there and try to pick off any Germans who might expose themselves. Lieut. Wallace said, however, that we had been ordered to go on at all costs.

At this, he stood up and within a few seconds dropped down riddled with bullets. This left me with the same problem and having observed his action, I felt that I must do the same. I stood up and was immediately hit by two bullets and dropped down . . .

I am now convinced that when it comes to the crunch, nobody has any fear at all.

DEPTH STUDY 2

How did women win the right to vote?

Through much of the history you have studied, women were treated as second-class citizens. Some might say they still are today. What do you think?

This depth study investigates one important step towards equality for women – when women were given the right to **vote** in **elections** for **parliament**. There is a risk that we take such rights for granted today, but it took many years of sometimes violent struggle for women to achieve that right.

The **campaign** was led by two groups of women: the **suffragists** and the **Suffragettes**.

■ You will discover the names of the women who fought to get the vote and equality for women.
■ You will find out what tactics they used.
■ You will find out how many years it took them to win the vote.
■ You will decide for yourself just how successful the fight for women's rights has been.

14

You will need

- pen or pencil
- scissors
- sheet of paper

There are five pages to this task

Have there been any famous women in history?

Your task

You have only five minutes to complete this task! You should work in pairs. You could try to have a boy and a girl in each pair.

1. Complete the chart below. On the left-hand side write down names of any **famous men** from history.

   On the right-hand side write down the names of any **famous women** from history.

   Here are a few names from history to start you off:

   Henry VIII, Queen Victoria, Adolf Hitler, Joan of Arc.

FAMOUS MEN	FAMOUS WOMEN

2. Which list is the longest?
3. Why do you think one list is longer than the other?

14

In the task on page 1 most people probably wrote a much longer list of famous men than famous women. Why is this?

As you know, history is all about people and about the past. But historians cannot write about absolutely everything that has happened in the past. So they write about the people and events from the past that they think are important. Most of the people that historians write about are men. Most of the events they record are about men too.

Your task

1. Examine the cartoon below.
2. Decide what you think the cartoonist is trying to say.

> 💬 **Do you agree with what the cartoonist is saying?**

Tutenkhamun Alexander the Great Julius Caesar Mohamed Alfred Robin Hood Saladin Marco Polo
Sophocles Abraham Hannibal Jesus Christ Charlemagne William the Conqueror St Francis

Wat Tyler Henry VII Martin Luther Guy Fawkes Samuel Pepys William Harvey Nelson Karl Marx Lenin Hitler
Richard III Henry VIII Francis Drake Oliver Cromwell Wolfe Tone Napoleon Wellington Mussolini Stalin

Another boring HIS Story lesson!

What about HER Story?

Even better . . . what about OUR Story?

14

☞

Your task

Work in pairs for this task.

💬 **Do YOU know the names of these women from history?**

You have been given some pictures and information about nine famous women from history. Below are their names.

- Helen of Troy
- Boudicca
- Margaret Thatcher

- Cleopatra
- Marie Curie
- Florence Nightingale

- Lady Godiva
- Queen Elizabeth I
- Marilyn Monroe

1. Match each picture to the right description.
2. Write the name of each woman under her picture.
3. Write her name and the date when she was famous on a large timeline like the one below.

name	
date	
Timeline of famous women from history	

4. Which three women do you think are the most famous?

   A. _____ B. _____ C. _____

5. Circle the words from the list below that you think describe WHY they became famous.

- they were royalty
- they were beautiful
- they had famous parents
- they were brave
- they got angry and tried to change things
- men fancied them

- they were just lucky
- they were very intelligent
- they tried to make things better for men and women
- they were stupid and were tricked by men

💬 **Do you think that the women from history became famous for different reasons from the men?**

Cut out and match these descriptions with the pictures on page 5.

In the 1100s she rode naked through the streets of Coventry because her husband was making the poor people pay too many taxes. Only one person, Peeping Tom, came out to stare at her.	In about 500BC, Trojan soldiers captured the most beautiful woman in Greece. She was a prisoner for twenty years until she was rescued by Odysseus who hid his soldiers in a wooden horse.	In AD61 she persuaded many tribes in Britain to rebel against the Romans who had raised taxes and raped her daughters. The rebels burned down Colchester and London. Eventually the Romans won so she took poison.
She was Britain's first woman Prime Minister. She governed from 1979 to 1990. She is sometimes known as the 'Iron Lady'.	In the late 1800s she was a famous scientist who helped to discover X-rays. She did not know that radiation causes cancer. Slowly she became very sick and died.	She was a famous film star in the 1950s. People say she was the most popular pin-up girl of all time. Eventually she became so unhappy she committed suicide.
She was Queen of England from 1558 to 1603. She never married because she didn't want her heart to rule her head. She had a few close advisers who were men. Her navy beat the Spanish Armada.	She was famous for helping wounded soldiers in 1854 during the Crimean War. She used to visit hospitals carrying a lamp. She would look after the wounded even when her own life was in danger.	In 31BC, before the Romans invaded Britain, this famous Queen of Egypt killed herself after her lover, Mark Antony, was defeated in battle by Octavius Caesar.

Cut out and match these pictures with the descriptions on page 4.

✂

15

You will need

- pen or pencil
- scissors
- A4 paper

How did the Suffragettes try to win the vote for women?

In 1800 most women in British society had little power or influence. When they got married, all their money and possessions belonged to their husband. Even if a woman had inherited a country house with land, she had to give it to her husband. Women were not allowed to become doctors or go to university. They were not allowed to vote in elections for parliament, and if a woman got divorced, she was unable to see her own children.

How did women try to change their situation?

During the nineteenth century, things began to improve a little. Women **campaigned** to change men's attitudes. They had some successes. In the 1860s they won the right to go to university. In the 1870s they won the right to become doctors. In the 1880s they

won the right to own their own houses and to keep the land they had inherited! But women were still not allowed to vote in elections even though women called the suffragists had campaigned for years to get the government to listen to them. They were called suffragists because they wanted universal suffrage. Universal suffrage means that all adults, whether male or female, rich or poor, are allowed to vote for parliament. They used peaceful methods such as petitions and meetings to campaign.

Who were the Suffragettes?

By 1903, some women became so frustrated that men wouldn't give them the vote that they decided to form a new organisation. They were called Suffragettes. This group was willing to use violent and aggressive methods to try and persuade people to listen to them. However, the group hoped that whatever tactics they used, no one would be physically hurt except perhaps themselves.

The leader of the Suffragettes was a woman called Emmeline Pankhurst.

SOURCE 1 Emmeline Pankhurst

THE TWENTIETH-CENTURY WORLD SUPPORT MATERIALS © JOHN MURRAY

15 page 2

☞

What did the Suffragettes do?

Emmeline Pankhurst had three daughters, Christabel, Sylvia and Adela. All three of them became members of the new group. They gave themselves a name, 'The Women's Social and Political Union' (nicknamed the Suffragettes). The group's slogan was 'Deeds not Words.'

For the next ten years the Suffragettes tried to get parliament to change the law and allow women to vote. They wanted publicity for their campaign so they got themselves arrested on purpose. They heckled at meetings and chained themselves to railings at the Houses of Parliament.

What happened to the Suffragettes?

Many Suffragettes went to prison. In July 1909, one prisoner called Marjorie Wallace Dunlop decided to go on hunger strike. She was protesting about the dreadful way that Suffragettes were treated in prison. Soon other Suffragettes began to copy her. The government didn't know what to do.

In the end it decided to force-feed the women. This was a cruel treatment which didn't really get enough food into the women's stomachs. The prisons would wait until the women were nearly starved to death and then release them. As soon as the women regained their health they were rearrested and sent back to prison.

Many people in Britain supported the Suffragettes. But still parliament would not give women the vote. Some Suffragettes became so cross that they started a more extreme campaign. They smashed windows, burned pillar boxes and bombed and burned buildings.

Your task 🔍 ✎

On page 3 there are three picture sources.

1. Which picture tells you **who** the Suffragettes were?

   Source _____ tells me that the Suffragettes were _____

   _____

2. Which picture tells you something about **what** the Suffragettes did?

   Source _____ tells me that the Suffragettes _____

   _____

3. Which picture tells you something about **what happened** to the Suffragettes?
   Source _____ tells me that the Suffragettes were _____

   _____

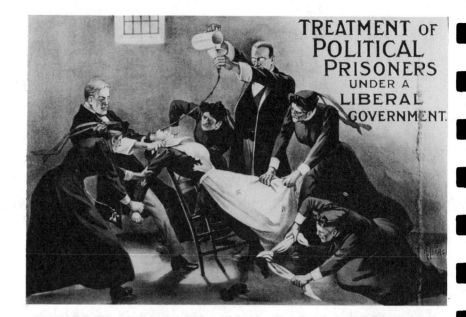

SOURCE 2 A poster showing what happened to Suffragettes when they were force-fed in prison

SOURCE 3 Leading Suffragettes meet to discuss their plans. From left to right: Flora Drummond, Christabel Pankhurst, Jessie Kenny, Mrs Nellie Martel, Emmeline Pankhurst, Mrs Charlotte Despard

SOURCE 4 Mrs Pankhurst is arrested after a Suffragette demonstration outside the Houses of Parliament

THE TWENTIETH-CENTURY WORLD SUPPORT MATERIALS © JOHN MURRAY

15

☞

Your task

Here are some more sources.

1. Cut out the sources.
2. Put them in chronological order.
3. Examine each source carefully.
4. Put the letter A next to the source which gives you most information about **who** the Suffragettes were.

   Put the letter B next to the source which gives you most information about **what** the Suffragettes did.

   Put the letter C next to the source which gives you most information about **what happened** to the Suffragettes.

SOURCE 5 From a newspaper report, 12 October 1909, on the force-feeding of Suffragettes in prison

A full inquiry is to be held into the treatment of a Suffragette Laura Ainsworth who was force-fed. She said:

   'I was raised into a sitting position and a tube about two feet long was produced. My mouth was opened with a steel instrument. I felt a choking sensation and a cork gag was placed between my teeth to keep my mouth open.'

SOURCE 6 From a newspaper report, 10 October 1903, on the formation of a new women's group

A number of women met in Manchester today to form a new militant movement to gain the vote. Their motto is 'Deeds not words'. Their leader is Mrs Emmeline Pankhurst who said membership is only for women – who can be from any political party as long as they want action.

SOURCE 7 From a newspaper article, 1 March 1912

Militant Suffragettes, many of them with stones and hammers hidden in their muffs, caused thousands of pounds worth of damage in a window-smashing rampage throughout the West End of London today.

SOURCE 8 From a newspaper article, 14 June 1913

Thousands of Suffragettes said a last sad farewell today to the woman they see as their martyred heroine – Emily Davison. She fell under the King's horse at the Derby ten days ago when she dashed into the path of the horse and tried to seize its reins.

SOURCE 9 Cartoon from *The Suffragette* newspaper showing two male doctors discussing a Suffragette's health!

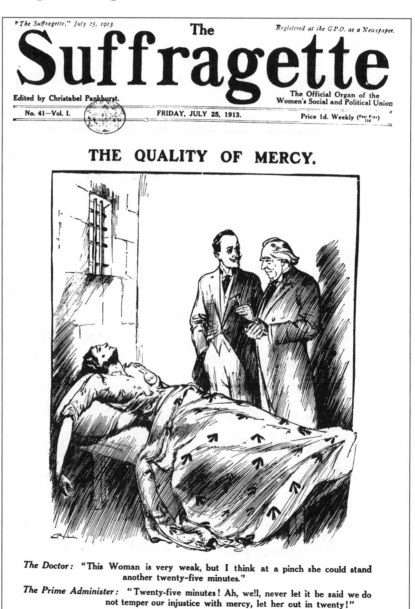

Why did the Suffragettes lose support?

For several years, between 1904 and 1910, the Suffragettes were extremely popular with hundreds of thousands of women, especially the middle classes. Many men supported them too. People were disgusted at the way they were treated in prison. People thought that force-feeding was inhumane.

Unfortunately, as the Suffragettes began to use more and more violent methods, attitudes began to change. People became angry at the vandalism. They got bored. Other things seemed to be more important. The government took hardly any notice. There were worrying things happening abroad with Germany and Austria–Hungary. By the end of 1912, the Suffragettes were losing public sympathy. The peaceful suffragists tried to save the campaign but it was a great struggle to win back support.

Your task

1. What would these two people have to say about the following events? Remember to look carefully at the dates.

A middle-class woman with a good education. She is married with three daughters

A middle-class man with a good education. He wants to become an MP

1908 Two Suffragettes chained themselves to the railings of No. 10 Downing Street. Five other Suffragettes tried to enter the House of Commons hidden in a furniture van.

1913 A Suffragette called Emily Wilding Davison threw herself under the king's horse at the Epsom Derby. She was killed.

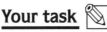
Your task ✎
You should work in pairs for this task.

1. Each pair is responsible for writing two articles for *The Suffragette* newspaper on page 8. One person should write the article as if it was 1908. In this article, you will explain:
   ■ who the Suffragettes are
   ■ what the two Suffragettes who tied themselves to the railings did
   ■ what is happening to the Suffragettes at this time
   ■ what people's attitudes to the Suffragettes are.

   The other person should write the article as if it was 1913. In this article you will explain:
   ■ what happened to Emily Davison
   ■ how the rest of the Suffragettes are feeling
   ■ why you are worried about people's attitudes to the Suffragettes
   ■ why, despite all the bad publicity, women should still support the 'cause'.

2. Design two of the following to go somewhere on the front page of your newspaper:
   ■ a slogan calling for votes for women
   ■ an advert selling the Suffragette ribbons
   ■ a poster condemning the government for its tactics on force-feeding
   ■ an invitation to a public meeting to discuss votes for women.

Use this page to write your article on the
Suffragettes as described on page 7.

The Suffragette

The Official Organ of the
Women's Social and Political Union

Edited by Christabel Pankhurst

Price 1d weekly

16

Why did women's jobs change during the First World War?

As soon as war with Germany was announced on 4 August 1914, the Suffragettes stopped their campaign. All Suffragette prisoners were released. Mrs Pankhurst changed the name of her party to 'The Woman's Party'. She changed the name of *The Suffragette* newspaper to *Britannia.* In 1915, she began to help the government by persuading women to join the war effort by working in the factories. Over one million women started work during the First World War.

Your task

1. Examine Sources 1–6 carefully and read any additional information.
2. Make a list of **all** the jobs that women did during the War:

_____ , _____ , _____ ,

_____ , _____ , _____ ,

_____ , _____ .

SOURCE 1 Women looked after the wounded soldiers in hospitals near the trenches. This is how one woman described her life:

We slept in our clothes and cut our hair short so that it would tuck inside our caps. Dressing meant simply putting on our boots . . . There were times when we had to scrape the lice off with the blunt edge of a knife and our underclothes stuck to us.

SOURCE 2 A munitions factory painted by E.F. Skinner

Other women went to work in the factories. These were not the usual cotton or clothing factories where women had always worked. They worked in factories which made guns, bullets and shells.

Thousands of women left their homes in the cities and began to work on farms producing food for the nation.

SOURCE 3 Tar sprayers resurfacing a road in London

SOURCE 4 A fitter at the London Bus Company in 1918

There were women bus drivers, women road builders and women who worked at coalmines. There were also women nurses, teachers, doctors and factory hands as there had been before the War.

SOURCE 5 Women workers at a Lancashire colliery in September 1918. The total workforce at this colliery was 9000, of whom 500 were women. They did not work underground, but did surface work such as sorting or carrying coal

SOURCE 6 In 1910 the Suffragettes published this postcard. It tried to persuade the government that women were doing much more sensible things than men. Yet they still weren't allowed to vote.

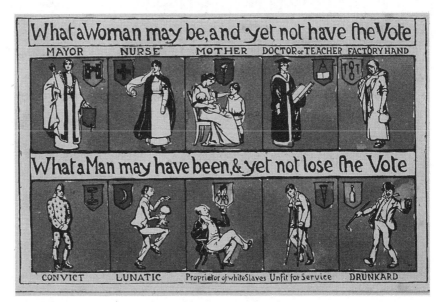

What a Woman may be, and yet not have the Vote

MAYOR   NURSE   MOTHER   DOCTOR or TEACHER   FACTORY HAND

What a Man may have been, & yet not lose the Vote

CONVICT   LUNATIC   Proprietor of white Slaves   Unfit for Service   DRUNKARD

☞

Your task

It is 1916. Britain has been at war for two years. Mrs Pankhurst has been asked to design a new postcard which will persuade even more women to go out to work. But she can't help herself. Even in the midst of war, Mrs Pankhurst is arguing that after the War women should be treated equally.

1. Use Sources 1–5 to illustrate the middle set of boxes.

2. Use your knowledge and understanding of the Suffragette Movement to complete the bottom section. You could write or draw your own ideas.

HOW WOMEN SERVED BRITAIN BEFORE THE WAR				
Mayor	Nurse	Mother	Doctor or Teacher	Factory Hand

HOW ARE WOMEN SERVING BRITAIN NOW

HOW WOMEN SHOULD BE ALLOWED TO SERVE BRITAIN AFTER THE WAR

Why did women get the vote in 1918?

You will need

- pen or pencil

In 1916 the government was thinking about changing the law so that soldiers fighting in the War would be able to vote in the General Election after the War. Women's groups decided to try to persuade the government to include them at the same time. This time they did succeed. In 1918 parliament finally passed a new law which gave all women aged over thirty the right to vote. Sources 1–4 give reasons why this happened.

Your task

On these two pages there are four sources. Each source gives you a reason why women got the vote in 1918.

1. Read each source carefully.

2. Give each source a mark out of 10:

   1 = a completely unimportant reason why women got the vote

   10 = a vital reason why women got the vote.

3. Explain your reasons for giving each mark.

VOTES FOR HEROINES AS WELL AS HEROES

SOURCE 1

A cartoon from the cover of *Votes for Women* magazine, 26 November 1915

marks out of 10 _____
reasons for giving this mark

_____

_____

SOURCE 2 E.S. Montague, Minister of Munitions, 1916

Women have proved themselves able to do work that before the War was seen as solely the work of men . . . Where is the man now who would deny to woman the civil rights which she has earned by her hard work?

marks out of 10 _____
reasons for giving this mark

_____

_____

_____

_____

SOURCE 3 A school textbook, 1996

In 1916 and 1917 there were no demonstrations, but there were many meetings between women's leaders and politicians, and a flood of telegrams and letters were sent to MPs.

SOURCE 4 Sylvia Pankhurst, 1931

People's memory of militancy, and the certainty that it would return if the claims of women were set aside, was a much stronger factor in overcoming the reluctance of those who would again have postponed giving women the vote.

marks out of 10 _____
reasons for giving this mark

_____

_____

_____

_____

_____

_____

_____

marks out of 10 _____
reasons for giving this mark

_____

_____

_____

_____

_____

_____

_____

 Which do you think was the most important reason why women over thirty eventually got the vote in 1918?

DEPTH STUDY 3
The rise of the dictators in Europe

♦ **HISTORY DICTIONARY**

The important words	My explanation of them
government	_____
dictatorship	_____
democracy	_____

Changes

The end of the First World War brought many changes. The biggest changes were in the ways that countries were governed. The War had changed the way people thought and felt. It had made many countries very poor. Eleven million men and women had died as a result of the War.

People from all over Europe began to ask questions about how the War had been allowed to happen. They began to blame their **governments** and their leaders who had started the War. They wanted things to change so that their lives would become better.

In some countries this just meant that different political parties became popular. More people were allowed to vote, but the ways of governing stayed the same. In other countries, people lost faith in the old ways of government.

In three of Europe's most powerful countries – Germany, Russia and Italy – dictators took power. A dictator has absolute control over his country. In the 1930s many people thought that countries could be ruled much better by **dictatorship** than by **democracy**. In this depth study you will find out why dictatorship was so attractive.

18

You will need

- a set of dictatorship cards
- glue

How are democracies and dictatorships different?

Between 1918, the end of the First World War, and 1939, the start of the Second World War, the countries of Europe began to divide into two sorts. Some were governed as democracies, the others were governed as dictatorships.

If you lived in a democracy, it meant that every adult could have a say in how the country was run. There was more than one political party. People could choose which of these parties ran the country by voting for it. But even the party that ran the country still had to listen to other people's points of view.

If you lived in a dictatorship, it meant that one person, the dictator, ruled the country and made all the decisions. The people had no say in how the country was run. The dictator told everybody else what to do and they had to obey him. If people didn't like what was happening they would have to keep quiet or else they would get into trouble.

How did democracies and dictatorships work?

On pages 2 and 3 there are six statements about how a democracy works.

Your task

1. Discuss each statement about democracies with your teacher. Make sure you all know what they mean.
2. Your teacher will give you six cards. On each card is a statement about how a dictatorship works. Read each card carefully. Each dictatorship statement can be paired with a democracy statement. Can you match the statements up? (The first one has been done for you.)
3. Glue the matching statement into the correct box.

> **From your knowledge about democracies and dictatorships, are we in Britain living in a democracy or a dictatorship?**

☞

How a democracy works

Stick the dictatorship cards into the correct boxes.

How a democracy works

Elections take place every few years so that people can change the government if they want to.

At elections the voters choose which political party will govern the country.

There is a range of political parties. It is legal to form new parties.

How a dictatorship works

There is only the dictator's political party. No other parties are allowed.

☞

How a democracy works

Stick the dictatorship cards into the correct boxes.

How a democracy works		How a dictatorship works	
J.C. ANNUAL CONGRE	People are free to belong to trade unions.		
F.A.C.E. Fight against Cuts in education / education cuts don't heal / MORE CASH FOR OUR KIDS	People are free to criticise the government as long as they don't break any laws.		
You were caught speeding Lord Melchet. I'm fining you £500. You should be ashamed of yourself, being a member of the aristocracy.	Everyone has to obey the law of the land.		

Dictatorship cards

Copy and cut up for each pupil.

There is only the dictator's political party. No other political parties are allowed.

Trade unions are banned.

Everyone except the leader of the country has to obey the law of the land.

If there are elections, voters can only vote for the dictator's party.

If anyone criticises the government they are put in prison.

Elections only happen if the dictator wants them, and the dictator can't be voted out.

19

You will need

- a set of pictures, speeches, slogans and fact files
- pen or pencil
- blue and red pens or pencils

♦ **HISTORY DICTIONARY**

The important words	My explanation of them
Fascism	_____
	_____
	_____
Nazism	_____
	_____
	_____
Communism	_____
	_____
	_____

Who were the European dictators?

Your task

1. Find out, first of all from a dictionary and then from discussions with your teacher, what the key words above mean.
2. Record your explanation in the right place.

The three most famous dictators in Europe were **Adolf Hitler**, **Josef Stalin** and **Benito Mussolini**. Each of them made sure that everybody living in his country obeyed his orders. They allowed people to vote for only one political party, theirs! In Italy it was called the **Fascist** party, in Germany it was called the **Nazi** party and in the USSR it was called the **Communist** party.

Some of the things that Fascists, Communists and Nazis believed in were the same. Others were completely different. For instance, whilst they all believed that there should be one strong leader and only one political party, **the Fascists and Nazis hated the Communists**. This was because Communists believed that all money and land should be shared equally between the people. Fascists and Nazis did not agree with this. They said that some people deserved more money because they worked harder. Often these people just happened to be friends of the Fascist or Nazi leader. It would probably be fair to say that **Fascist and Nazi beliefs were almost identical.** In other words, the Nazis were Fascists too!

Your task

Copy these labels into the correct boxes on the outline map below.

  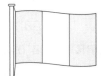  

German flag   USSR flag   Italian flag   Communist symbol   Fascist symbol   Nazi symbol

Name	Symbol	Flag

Outline map of Europe – the three main dictatorships

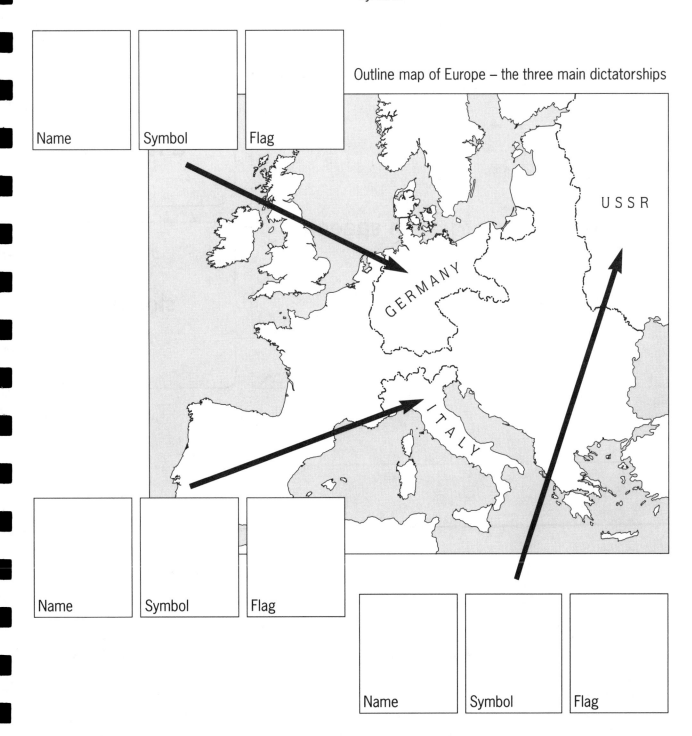

Name	Symbol	Flag

Name	Symbol	Flag

☞

Your task

You should work in groups of three for this task. You will need:

■ one set of pictures, speeches, fact files and slogans from your teacher.

It is November 1936. You have just been recruited by MI6 as a new secret service agent. Your job is to organise the files on the three most famous European dictators. Unfortunately, the previous agent turned out to be a spy. He has deliberately muddled up all the files to confuse you.

Sort all the documents into three files, one for Adolf Hitler, one for Josef Stalin and one for Benito Mussolini.

For each dictator you will need

a portrait

a speech

a fact file

slogans

Copy for each group of pupils.

A propaganda portrait showing Adolf Hitler standing triumphantly in front of adoring crowds.

A well-known portrait of Benito Mussolini. His people know him as 'Il Duce', the leader. The artist has naturally drawn his black shirt – one of Mussolini's favourite symbols of Fascist power.

This portrait is of Josef Stalin who is known to many as 'The Man of Steel'. No one has ever seen him without his huge moustache.

MUSSOLINI, B.

Full name: **BENITO MUSSOLINI**
(also known as 'Il Duce' – the leader)

Subject: SPEECH MADE BY BENITO MUSSOLINI – ROME JULY 1936

I send greetings to all my faithful followers.
I am Il Duce, your great leader. I am like a god.
I have done so much for all the Italian people.

I have made the rich men happy because they have been able to keep their businesses and their land. They can make a good profit. But my Fascist government controls what happens to most of the money. We make lots of money because I have banned all strikes. The rich men are also happy because all my followers who wear 'blackshirts' are violent and strong. They beat up all those workers who don't like the system.

Everyone is happy about the new roads I have built.
This helps the farmers to grow more food.
Don't forget, I have also set up new industries and built electric dams.

The Roman Catholic Church is on my side because I have made it the official religion of Italy. This means that all the priests will tell people to support the Fascists. This also means that men can tell their wives to stay at home and produce beautiful Fascist babies. The Roman Catholic Church likes these new laws of mine.

I hate everyone who prefers peaceful ways of sorting out an argument. I hate all Jews, Black people or anyone who is weak or disabled. I admire what Hitler is doing to these people. No one dares to go against me.

There is only one political party, the Fascists!

Copy for each group of pupils.

STALIN, J.

Full name: **JOSEF STALIN**
(also known as 'The Man of Steel')

Subject: SPEECH MADE BY JOSEF STALIN – 1936

To all loyal Russian Communists, I send greetings.

Only one political party will ever be allowed in this country. The Communist Party looks after everyone. Never forget this. A few foolish people have disagreed with me in the past. But I soon got rid of them. At the last count, I think it was eight million people who have been executed.

I have had statues of myself put up in every town. In the old days people starved to death. Now I make rich and poor people work together. We share food between the country farmers, the peasants and the city workers. This means that when the crops didn't grow in 1933, only five million peasants died. You see what a great ruler I am?

We Communists look after everyone, even those who can't work or are sick. Just to make sure of this, I have taken over all the factories in this country. I know these are countries like Britain who don't like this, but that is because they want to keep all the profits themselves. Our Communist system is much better.

So remember, the harder you all work, the sooner we can build hospitals and schools for the whole country.

All power to the Soviets!

Copy for each group of pupils.

HITLER, A.

Full name: **ADOLF HITLER**
(also known as 'the Führer' – the leader)

Subject: SPEECH MADE BY ADOLF HITLER AT A NAZI YOUTH
RALLY IN BERLIN SEPTEMBER 1936

I am the greatest leader of all time. I have great plans. Soon I will make
sure that all the land which once belonged to Germany is returned.

I hate all Communists, Jews, Black people, homosexuals and gypsies. So
I have taken their jobs and given them to true Germans who have blond
hair and blue eyes. Only the German Aryan Master Race can become
true German citizens.

I am sending all non-Germans to concentration camps. I have built
factories to make weapons. So there is no longer any unemployment in
Germany. This is all thanks to me, the one true ruler.

Soon there will be a special German church where the bible is replaced
by my book called <u>Mein Kampf (My Struggle)</u>. The cross will be replaced
by a sword. Women will not be allowed to work. They will cook, have
children and go to church.

Young people of Germany, the future is yours!

Heil Hitler!

fact file: Benito Mussolini

- Leader of the Italian Fascists
- Born 1883, son of a blacksmith
- A violent bully at school, he joined the Communist Party before the First World War. Sometimes ended up in prison because of the strikes he led
- Fought bravely in the First World War and was badly wounded. Loved the violence and danger
- Left the Communist Party after the War. Set up the Fascist Party in 1919
- His Fascist Party won the elections in 1922
- Has been a dictator since 1925 when he made himself Head of Government
- Makes laws without consulting other people

Fascist slogans

'Believe! Obey! Fight!'

'Better to live one day like a lion than a hundred years like a sheep.'

'A minute on the battlefield is worth a lifetime of peace.'

'War is to man as childbirth is to women.'

Copy for each group of pupils.

fact file: Josef Stalin

- Leader of the Russian (USSR) Communist Party since 1925
- Born 1879
- Dreadfully scarred with smallpox on his face
- A convicted bank robber who spent four years in jail in Siberia
- Brutally murders anyone who disagrees with him, even his own friends in the Communist Party
- Wife has recently committed suicide because of his brutal behaviour

Communist slogans

'Peace, bread and land.'

'All power to the Soviets.'

fact file: Adolf Hitler

- Leader of the NAZI Party
  (National Socialist German Workers Party)
- Born in Austria in 1889
- Won medal for bravery in First World War
- Became leader of the Nazi Party in 1920
- Tried to seize power in 1923 and spent time in prison for this
- In 1924 he wrote *Mein Kampf* (*My Struggle*). This shows how much he hates the Jews
- Has been dictator of Germany since 1933

Nazi slogans

'Germany must be ruled by a single strong leader who has great power – a Führer.'

'The weak must be chiselled away. I want young men and women who can suffer pain.'

'A young German must be as swift as a greyhound, as tough as leather and as hard as Krupp's steel.'

~~~~~~

☞

What did the dictators believe in?

Your task A

Still in groups of three, each person should work on one of the dictators.

For this task, you will need all the information in the file of your dictator.

Use your Confidential Report sheet on page 5.

1. Write the name, age and country of your chosen dictator in the correct place.
2. Use the picture to draw his likeness.
3. Use the picture and his fact file to write a description of him.
4. Use the fact file to find out about his criminal record.
5. Now tell your friends what you know about your dictator.

Your task B

Keep working on the same dictator.

To do this task you will need:

■ the Political Record sheet on page 6
■ the speech by your dictator.

1. Read the speech by your dictator. Make sure you understand everything that has been written. Ask your teacher to help you if there is something you don't understand.
2. Underline in blue all the things which tell you what your dictator has done.
3. Underline in red all the things which tell you what your dictator believed in.
4. Record them in note form in the correct column of your Political Record sheet.
5. Think about what you have just read and written. Decide which TWO things your dictator either DID or BELIEVED IN which, in your opinion, PROVE that he was a dictator.
6. Record these at the bottom of your Political Record sheet.
7. Now tell your friends what your dictator believed in.

 From what you have found out, which of the three dictators was the most dangerous and why?

Confidential Report: The European Dictators

name

_____

age

_____

country he rules over

_____

photofit likeness of

_____

description of _____

_____

_____

_____

_____

_____ 's **criminal record**

_____

_____

_____

_____

Political Record of _____

Things _____ has done   Things _____ believes in

_____   _____

_____   _____

_____   _____

_____   _____

_____   _____

_____   _____

_____   _____

The two main things which _____ **did or believes in which I think PROVE that he is a dictator**

_____

_____

_____

_____

The reasons why I think they prove he is a dictator are _____

_____

_____

_____

_____

DEPTH STUDY 4
Hitler's rise to power

<table>
<tr><td colspan="2">◆ HISTORY DICTIONARY</td></tr>
<tr><td>The important words</td><td>My explanation of them</td></tr>
<tr><td>economy</td><td>_____</td></tr>
<tr><td></td><td>_____</td></tr>
<tr><td></td><td>_____</td></tr>
<tr><td>inflation</td><td>_____</td></tr>
<tr><td></td><td>_____</td></tr>
<tr><td></td><td>_____</td></tr>
<tr><td>unemployment</td><td>_____</td></tr>
<tr><td></td><td>_____</td></tr>
<tr><td></td><td>_____</td></tr>
</table>

After the government of Germany had signed the Treaty of Versailles in 1919, life became even worse for ordinary German people than it had been during the War. Germany had to pay such enormous fines to the countries that had won the War that there wasn't enough money left to pay decent wages. Not only had Germany lost the War, and so lost its pride, but also it had lost its **economy**. There was high **inflation**. This means that prices rose so much that people could not afford to buy even basic things like food. Many people were starving.

For the next fifteen years Germany faced one crisis after another. The country went bankrupt. There were strikes and massive **unemployment**. It seemed that the government could do nothing about it. Adolf Hitler, however, persuaded the German people that he could solve the problems.

In this depth study you will look at:
- Hitler's rise to power during Germany's economic problems.
- How he was able to become leader of Germany.
- How Hitler set about taking over the rest of Europe.

20

There are two pages to this task

You will need

- pen or pencil
- a Treaty of Versailles terms sheet

◆ HISTORY DICTIONARY

The important words	My explanation of them
President	_____
	_____
Prime Minister	_____
	_____
treaty	_____
	_____
League of Nations	_____
	_____

Why was the Treaty of Versailles so unpopular in Germany?

The First World War ended in November 1918. The people of Germany and Austria had lost. The people of Britain, France, the USA had won.

A few months later, the **President** of America and the **Prime Ministers** of Britain and France met. Their aim was to make Germany pay for what had happened in the War. So they made a **treaty** between themselves. This has become known as the Treaty of Versailles. No one from Germany or Austria–Hungary was allowed to come to the meetings because they had lost the War. They just had to agree to the treaty and sign all the papers. Germany was not allowed to join the **League of Nations**. (This was an organisation joined by many countries from all over the world. Its aim was to solve any disagreements between countries peacefully.)

Your task

Your teacher will give you a worksheet with three columns.

In the centre column are all the 'terms' of the Treaty of Versailles. (Terms means all the things that countries who signed the treaty had to agree to do.)

1. It is 1923. The War has been over for five years. Write down in the left-hand column what you think an ordinary British person would have thought about each of the terms of the treaty. Write down in the right-hand column what an ordinary German person would have thought about each of the terms of the treaty. (The first one has been done for you.)

2. Discuss what you have written with a partner. Between you, decide whether you think the Treaty of Versailles was fair or unfair to the Germans.

3. On page 2 write a paragraph explaining your views.

Terms of the Treaty of Versailles

Copy this sheet to A3 size, one for each pupil.

GERMAN VIEWPOINT	TERMS OF THE TREATY	BRITISH VIEWPOINT				
It's not fair. Britain should take some of the blame. They wanted to try out their new ships, and to show us how useful their colonies were. I have lost my father and a cousin in the War.	1. Germany must accept the blame for starting the War.	That's exactly how it should be. I lost two brothers in the War. Kaiser Bill was determined to fight from the moment he started building all those new weapons. I hate the Germans.				
	2. Germany must get rid of most of its army and navy.					
	3. All German colonies to be taken away and given to Britain, France and other countries.					
	4. A League of Nations is set up to discuss problems rather than fight about them. Germany isn't allowed to join it.					
	5. Germany has to give some of its land to France, Poland, Belgium, Denmark and the League of Nations.					
	6. Germany is forbidden to unite with Austria.					
	7. Germany is forced to pay more than £6,600 million in fines to Britain, France and the other countries that won the War.					

Use this sheet to explain your views on the Treaty of Versailles.

WAS THE TREATY OF VERSAILLES FAIR?

In my opinion, the Treaty of Versailles was _____ to the Germans.

The reasons why I think this are _____

_____

_____

_____

_____

_____

_____

_____

_____

_____

_____

_____

_____

You will need
• pen or pencil

What was life like in Germany in 1923?

◆ **HISTORY DICTIONARY**

The important words	My explanation of them
inflation	_____

By 1923, Hans Oppenheimer had realised his dream. He was studying philosophy at Heidelberg University. Life was quite tough because there wasn't much money for food, lodgings or books. So every few weeks Hans wrote home to his parents in Nuremberg, to tell them how he was getting on and to stop them from worrying too much. You can see the envelopes from his letters on page 2.

Your task

Look carefully at the cost of the stamps for Hans' letters on page 2.
Now answer the following questions.

1. In May 1923, it cost 100 Deutschmarks to send a letter home.
   How much did it cost on:

   ■ 26 September 1923 _____

   ■ 24 October 1923 _____

   ■ 16 November 1923? _____

2. If a loaf of bread cost 100 Deutschmarks in May 1923, how much would a family have to pay for the same loaf of bread in July 1923?

   The family would have to pay _____

If a pound of sausages cost 100 Deutschmarks in May 1923 (about 25p in English money) they would have cost 100,000,000,000 (or one hundred billion) Deutschmarks on 16 November 1923. This would have been about £2,500,000 in English money. That means, the sausages would have cost two million, five hundred thousand pounds!

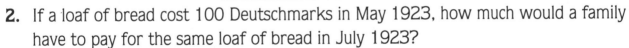

> **How do you think the following people would have felt about the economic crisis in Germany?**
> ■ A German housewife with four children
> ■ A German banker
> ■ A member of the German government
> ■ Adolf Hitler

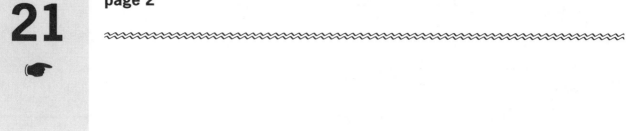

21 MAY 1923
(1 HUNDRED)
100 DM
1

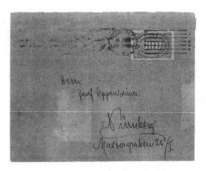

14 JULY '23
(3 HUNDRED)
300 DM
2

12 AUGUST
(1 THOUSAND)
1,000 DM
3

26 SEPTEMBER
(250 THOUSAND)
250,000 DM
4

5 OCTOBER
(2 MILLION)
2,000,000 DM
5

14 OCTOBER
(5 MILLION)
5,000,000 DM
6

24 OCTOBER
(10 MILLION)
10,000,000 DM
7

2 NOVEMBER
(150 MILLION)
150,000,000 DM
8

16 NOVEMBER
(10 MILLIARDEN)
10,000,000,000 DM
9

☞ When prices are like this it is called hyperinflation. It damages a country. People lose confidence. It particularly damages middle-class people with money saved up. Imagine if they had a million Deutschmarks in a bank in early 1923. They would be rich enough to buy a house with it. By the end of 1923 it would not buy even a cup of coffee.

Inflation was only one of Germany's problems in 1923. Another was that in a part of Germany called the Ruhr all the factories and mines were on strike. The French had taken over the factories because Germany had stopped paying fines to France. Another problem was that some political groups in Germany wanted a revolution. One of these groups was the Nazi Party, led by Adolf Hitler. The Nazis blamed the Treaty of Versailles, the Jews and the Communists for everything that was wrong with Germany.

Like most German people in 1924, Hans knew very little about Adolf Hitler or his beliefs. All he knew was that a madman called Hitler had been caught trying to take over the government of Germany.

Hans was sure Germany would survive these problems. He was hoping to get married to a fellow student of philosophy called Rita. He had a job lined up in the Jewish bank in Berlin, the capital of Germany. Hans was sure that the economic situation would improve and that things would slowly get better in Germany.

☞

<u>**Your task**</u>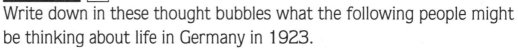
Write down in these thought bubbles what the following people might be thinking about life in Germany in 1923.

A German housewife
with four children

A German banker

A member of
the German government

Adolf Hitler

You will need

- pen or pencil
- a copy of
  Peace & War

♦ **HISTORY DICTIONARY**

The important words	My explanation of them
Chancellor	_____
	_____

How did Hitler become Chancellor in 1933?

Hans Oppenheimer and other people like him were completely wrong about Adolf Hitler. Within a few years of getting out of prison, Hitler had made the Nazis one of the most popular parties in Germany. Slowly but surely, more and more people began voting for Hitler in elections. Everywhere you went, you could read about Adolf Hitler and how he blamed the Jews. Finally, in the German elections of 1933, Hitler won enough votes to become the new **Chancellor** of Germany. He was now in charge.

Your task

You should work in pairs for this task.
You should use the two timelines on pages 4 and 5.

The timelines will help you to understand how Hitler was able to take over Germany.
■ One of you should read the timeline of events in Germany after the First World War.
■ The other person should read the timeline of Adolf Hitler's life.
As you read them, make sure you understand everything that you have read. You should also make sure that you have noticed the dates when things happened.
■ Now discuss with each other the following questions. You will need to use the knowledge you have each gained to answer the questions. Share your knowledge and then write down the answer you have agreed upon.

1. Why did people dislike the new German government in 1919?

_____

_____

_____

☞

2. When was Adolf Hitler born, and why did he win the Iron Cross?

_____

_____

_____

3. How do we know that by 1923 German money was useless?

_____

_____

_____

_____

4. Who did the Nazis blame for losing the First World War?

_____

_____

_____

5. Why do you think some German people would particularly hate French people during this period?

_____

_____

_____

6. Why was Hitler sent to jail in 1923?

_____

_____

7. What did Hitler do in jail?

_____

_____

8. Why would many Germans have agreed with Hitler's book, *Mein Kampf*?
   (You will both be able to think of several reasons for this.)

_____

_____

_____

9. Why did so many Germans vote for Hitler in the 1932 elections?
   (You will both be able to think of several reasons for this.)

_____

_____

_____

Timeline of events in Germany after the First World War

When the Germans surrendered in **1918**, Kaiser (Emperor) Wilhelm fled to Holland. People didn't like the new government. This was because in 1919 the government signed the Treaty of Versailles.

In **1922** the Germans found that they couldn't afford to pay the fines for war damage. So, in **1923**, the French invaded the Ruhr, part of Germany, and took over the coalfields. Thousands of Germans went on strike.

Germany was in chaos. German money lost nearly all its value. People used wheelbarrows to carry their wages home. Even then, a wheelbarrow full of money wasn't enough to buy a cup of coffee.

1924–1929. A new government got Germany back in order. It sorted out the money crisis and was even allowed to join the League of Nations. Then just as things were going well the whole world went into a Depression. Millions of Germans lost their jobs.

By **1932** Adolf Hitler's Nazi Party had become more and more popular because people thought Hitler could solve Germany's unemployment problems. People from all over Germany began to vote for him. By 1932, the Nazi Party was the largest party in the German parliament.

In **1933** Adolf Hitler became Chancellor of Germany. The Nazi reign of terror began.

THE TWENTIETH-CENTURY WORLD SUPPORT MATERIALS © JOHN MURRAY

☞

Timeline of Adolf Hitler's life

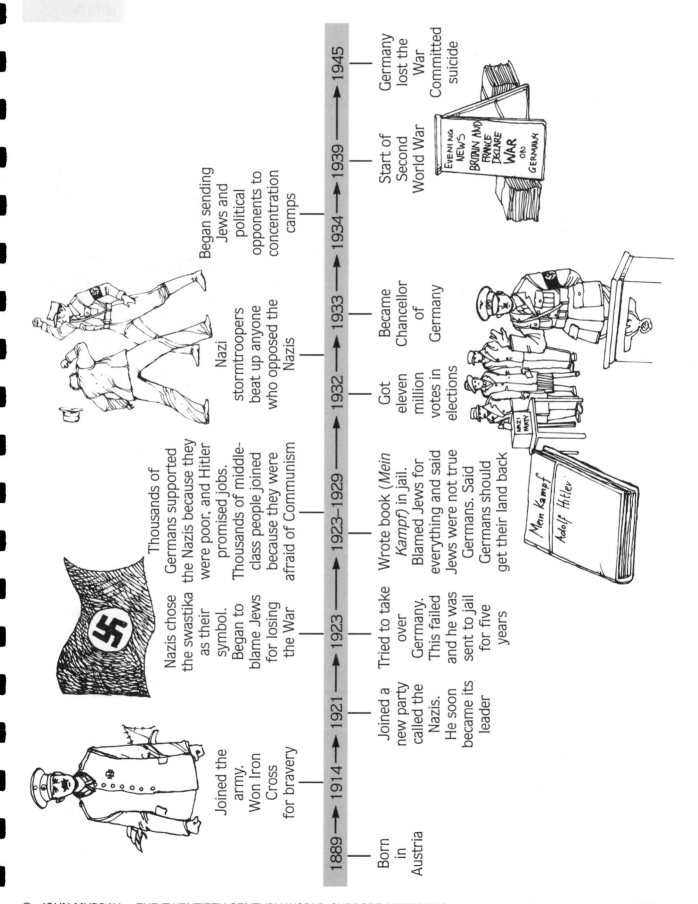

1889 — Born in Austria

1914 — Joined the army. Won Iron Cross for bravery

1921 — Joined a new party called the Nazis. He soon became its leader

1923 — Nazis chose the swastika as their symbol. Began to blame Jews for losing the War

Tried to take over Germany. This failed and he was sent to jail for five years

1923–1929 — Thousands of Germans supported the Nazis because they were poor, and Hitler promised jobs. Thousands of middle-class people joined because they were afraid of Communism

Wrote book (*Mein Kampf*) in jail. Blamed Jews for everything and said Jews were not true Germans. Said Germans should get their land back

1932 — Got eleven million votes in elections

1933 — Nazi stormtroopers beat up anyone who opposed the Nazis

Became Chancellor of Germany

1934 — Began sending Jews and political opponents to concentration camps

1939 — Start of Second World War

1945 — Germany lost the War Committed suicide

23

You will need
- pen or pencil

♦ HISTORY DICTIONARY

The important words	My explanation of them
extremist	_____
	_____

Why did Hitler rise to power?
Using the evidence

You have read what happened in Germany between 1918 and 1933. The question that historians have been asking ever since is 'Why did German people allow an **extremist** who believed in violence and terror to become Chancellor of Germany?'

<u>Your task</u>
Use the following sources of evidence to help you answer these questions.

SOURCE 1 German children playing with worthless bank notes, a photograph taken in 1923

1. Why do you think this photograph was taken?

_____

_____

_____

_____

2. How might people in Germany have felt when they saw the photograph?

_____

_____

_____

_____

☞

SOURCE 2 Graph showing how unemployment in Germany, Britain and the USA rose between 1929 and 1932

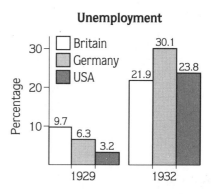

Unemployment

3. Examine Source 2 carefully.
   Which country had the highest rate of unemployment in 1932?

   _____

4. How would that make the people of Germany feel?

   _____

   _____

   _____

5. Read Source 3. Underline all the good things that Albert Speer thought Hitler would do for the country.

6. Choose what you think were the two most important things Hitler could offer. Write them out below.

   (i) _____

   _____

   (ii) _____

   _____

7. How do you think some adults in Germany might have felt when they read Albert Speer's description of Hitler's speech?

   _____

   _____

   _____

SOURCE 3
A description by Albert Speer, a Nazi, after he heard Hitler speaking in 1931

Here was hope. Here were new ideals.

The danger of Communism could be stopped, Hitler said, and instead of hopeless unemployment Germany could move towards economic recovery.

It was at this time that my mother saw a parade of stormtroopers [Hitler's private army]. The sight of such discipline in a time of chaos, and the impression of energy and hope, seems to have won her over.

☞

SOURCE 4 Graph showing unemployment in Germany from 1928 to 1933 and the seats won in the German parliament (the Reichstag) by the Nazis during the same period

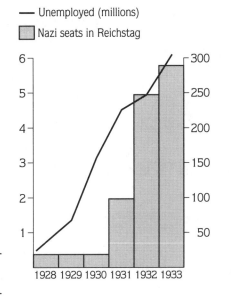

— Unemployed (millions)

☐ Nazi seats in Reichstag

8. How do we know that, as unemployment got worse, Hitler's Nazi Party became more and more popular?

_____

_____

_____

_____

_____

_____

9. Read this summary of Hitler's ideas in column 1 of the chart below. It comes from his book, _Mein Kampf_. Hitler wrote this book whilst he was in prison.
In blank column 2 write down why people in Germany would have liked these ideas in 1932. (The first one has been done for you.)

SOURCE 5 The ideas in _Mein Kampf_	Why people in Germany would have liked them
The Treaty of Versailles must be cancelled and land taken from the Germans must be returned.	They would like this because it meant that the land that had once been German would belong to Germany again. They would think about the crops they could grow on the land, the houses they could build and the businesses they could develop. They would hope that unemployed people could find jobs on this land.

The Germans are the 'Master Race'. They must keep themselves pure. Only those of German blood may be citizens. No Jews may be members of the nation. It was Jews who helped bring about Germany's defeat in the First World War. They must be destroyed.	
We demand land and colonies to feed our people and to house surplus population.	
We demand a strong central government led by a single leader, a Führer.	
All the people of German blood (including people living in Czechoslovakia and Austria) must be allowed to live in Germany.	

Now that you have answered all the questions, discuss with your teacher and the rest of the class why you think Adolf Hitler was allowed to become Chancellor of Germany.

24

You will need

- pen or pencil
- an atlas with a 1930s map of Europe

How did Hitler take control of most of Europe, 1936–1941?

From the moment Adolf Hitler became Chancellor of Germany in 1933, he was determined to make his country larger and more powerful. From 1936 to the beginning of the Second World War, Hitler's army took over other areas and countries. The people who lived there had to accept Nazi rules. During the Second World War Hitler invaded many other countries in Europe.

On page 2 is the story of how it happened.

Your task

When you have read the story of how Adolf Hitler took control of most of Europe, record the name of each country and the date it was invaded on one tentacle of the 'Hitler Octopus chart' below.

1919	1929	1936

After Germany lost the First World War, the countries that had won made the Germans suffer by taking money and land from them. Germany was only allowed to have a small army. This made the German people very angry. Many of them also became extremely poor.	Adolf Hitler and his Nazi Party persuaded millions of German people to vote for them. He blamed the Jews for losing the War. He promised people that he would give them jobs and food.	When Hitler had been Chancellor of Germany for three years, he decided to put his soldiers back in the Rhineland. This had been forbidden after the First World War.

1938	1938	1939

Hitler marched his soldiers into Austria and said he was the new leader. Many Austrians wanted to be part of Germany so they thought this was a good thing.	A few months later Hitler invaded Czechoslovakia. Other countries still did nothing to stop him. The British said Czechoslovakia was too far away to worry about.	Then Hitler invaded Poland. The rest of Europe began to get very worried. Britain and France declared war on Germany on 3 September 1939. But Hitler seemed to be unstoppable. He invaded Holland, France, Belgium, Norway and Denmark, all in the same year. Most people thought it was only a matter of time before he invaded Great Britain.

☞

Your task
It is 1940. Hitler's armies are moving quickly into other countries.
They have just taken over France, Holland and Belgium.
Write down what you think the following people would be feeling.

An ordinary British teenager

_____

_____

_____

_____

_____

_____

An ordinary German teenager

_____

_____

_____

_____

_____

_____

A young Polish Jew

_____

_____

_____

_____

_____

_____

An ordinary French teenager

_____

_____

_____

_____

_____

_____

DEPTH STUDY 5

The Home Front in the Second World War

♦ **HISTORY DICTIONARY**

The important words	My explanation of them
civilians	_____ _____
Blitz	_____ _____
evacuation	_____ _____
morale	_____ _____

The Second World War was the deadliest and most costly war the world had ever known. Around the world over thirty million people – most of them **civilians** – were killed. Britain's cities were hit by the **Blitz** which killed hundreds of thousands of people. Families were disrupted as children were sent away to the countryside to escape the bombing. This was called **evacuation**. Yet despite that, the **morale** of people at home did not collapse. Many talk about the War as a good time when families and communities worked together to help one another and to defeat the Germans.

In this depth study you will:

■ Investigate what life was like on the Home Front during the War.

■ Look at the experience of the O'Connor family whom you have already met. Their family was affected by many of the changes which the War caused.

■ Find out what it was like to be evacuated.

■ Find out what it was like for people in the Blitz.

25

You will need
• pen or pencil

Living through the War 1939–1945:
The O'Connor family preparing for the worst:
September 1939

The O'Connor family still lived in Liverpool at number 10 Jubilee Avenue. Three more children had been born to James and Elizabeth after the First World War – Joan, Tony and Frank. James still worked in insurance, but he was helped by two of his daughters, Kay and Joan.

Life had been good to the O'Connors. Molly, James, Louis and Winifred were happily married. All four of them had gone back to live in Seacombe where James and Elizabeth had met. Every Sunday the family would take a trip across the River Mersey to visit them. With four children still at home, Elizabeth was kept very busy. Of course there were no servants now, but Kay and Joan helped with the housework when they got home from work.

On 3 September 1939, Britain and France declared war on Germany. James and Elizabeth were not at all surprised. They had been expecting something like this for months. Elizabeth had been busy making blackout curtains for all the windows, whilst James, Tony and Frank had been helping Mr Yates to build an air-raid shelter at the end of his garden. It was brick-built and Mr Yates had insisted that the roof be made of solid concrete.

'Everyone in the avenue can use this shelter,' he said proudly. 'Hitler's bombers won't destroy this in a hurry!' Frank and Tony were curious.

'Why would Adolf Hitler want to bomb Liverpool, Mr Yates?' asked Tony.

At first, Mr Yates didn't reply. Instead he picked up a piece of paper and began drawing on it. 'See if you can work it out for yourselves,' he said to the two boys. 'Look at these pictures. If you can come up with five good reasons why Hitler should want to bomb Liverpool, I'll give you threepence pocket money!'

Your task

1. Examine the drawings made by Mr Yates. Each one represents a reason why Hitler might want to bomb Liverpool.
2. Try to work out what each reason is.
3. Record your reason in the box next to each picture and help Tony and Frank to win threepence extra pocket money!

Mr Yates' drawings	Reason why Hitler would want to bomb Liverpool
 MUNITIONS FACTORY	
TO THE LIVERPOOL DOCKS — TO BIRMINGHAM, COVENTRY AND LONDON	
Atlantic Ocean — Ireland — Norway and Sweden — Liverpool — USA — Spain and Africa	
HMS LIVERPOOL	
MERCHANT NAVY — FLOUR — This lot's come from the USA mate! You're to drive it down to Cornwall. — ARMY SUPPLIES VEHICLE	

☞

On 1 September 1939, two days before war was finally declared, the blackout was introduced. Elizabeth was so glad that she was prepared. It took less than two hours for the boys to help her put up the new curtains.

'Don't worry, boys,' she said, 'This is only a precaution. Maybe we won't declare war at all.'

Everyone knew that this was a faint hope.

Sure enough, two days later, war was declared and the whole family was issued with gas masks. They had to be taken everywhere. The smell of rubber and disinfectant made people sick. There were also some official instructions to go with the masks. Frank found these even more frightening than the mask itself!

Your task

1. Look at the leaflet (right) which was sent to every household in Britain.

2. Label all the things on this leaflet that might have made Frank worried or frightened.

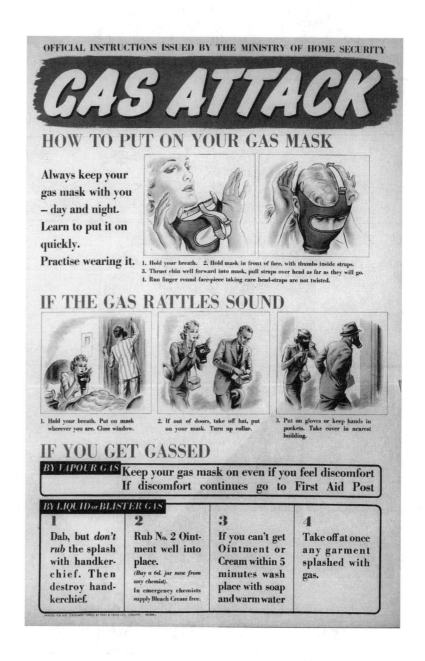

OFFICIAL INSTRUCTIONS ISSUED BY THE MINISTRY OF HOME SECURITY

GAS ATTACK

HOW TO PUT ON YOUR GAS MASK

Always keep your gas mask with you – day and night. Learn to put it on quickly. Practise wearing it.

1. Hold your breath.   2. Hold mask in front of face, with thumbs inside straps.
3. Thrust chin well forward into mask, pull straps over head as far as they will go.
4. Run finger round face-piece taking care head-straps are not twisted.

IF THE GAS RATTLES SOUND

1. Hold your breath. Put on mask wherever you are. Close window.

2. If out of doors, take off hat, put on your mask. Turn up collar.

3. Put on gloves or keep hands in pockets. Take cover in nearest building.

IF YOU GET GASSED

BY VAPOUR GAS Keep your gas mask on even if you feel discomfort
If discomfort continues go to First Aid Post

BY LIQUID or BLISTER GAS

1	2	3	4
Dab, but *don't rub* the splash with handkerchief. Then destroy handkerchief.	Rub No. 2 Ointment well into place. *(Buy a 6d. jar now from any chemist).* In emergency chemists supply Bleach Cream free.	If you can't get Ointment or Cream within 5 minutes wash place with soap and warm water	Take off at once any garment splashed with gas.

PRINTED FOR H.M. STATIONERY OFFICE BY POSH & CROSS LTD., LONDON.   (51/504.)

You will need
- an atlas
- pen or pencil

◆ **HISTORY DICTIONARY**

The important words	My explanation of them
evacuation	_____
	_____

Evacuation: we're going to the country

Everybody knew that Hitler would send his bombers to try and destroy the big cities where most of the industries were. The government decided to move people from these cities to safer parts of the country. This was called **evacuation**. During September 1939, over 1.5 million people were evacuated from the cities to small towns and villages in the countryside. These people were mostly women and children. Teachers were evacuated too, so that children could continue with their lessons!

Your task

1. Look at the map you have been given. The dots represent all the major cities in Britain. Find their names in your atlas and write them on or around the edge of the map.

2. The shaded areas represent all the places where tools, weapons, tanks and aeroplanes were being made. They are all close to large cities. Why do you think this was the case?

_____

_____

3. What do you think was the most dangerous part of the country to be living in in 1939?

_____

4. If you were James and Elizabeth, would you want your two sons to stay at home? Explain your answer.

_____

_____

5. Look carefully at the map of Great Britain again. Where do you think the people of Liverpool would send their children so that they would be safe but not too far away from home?

_____

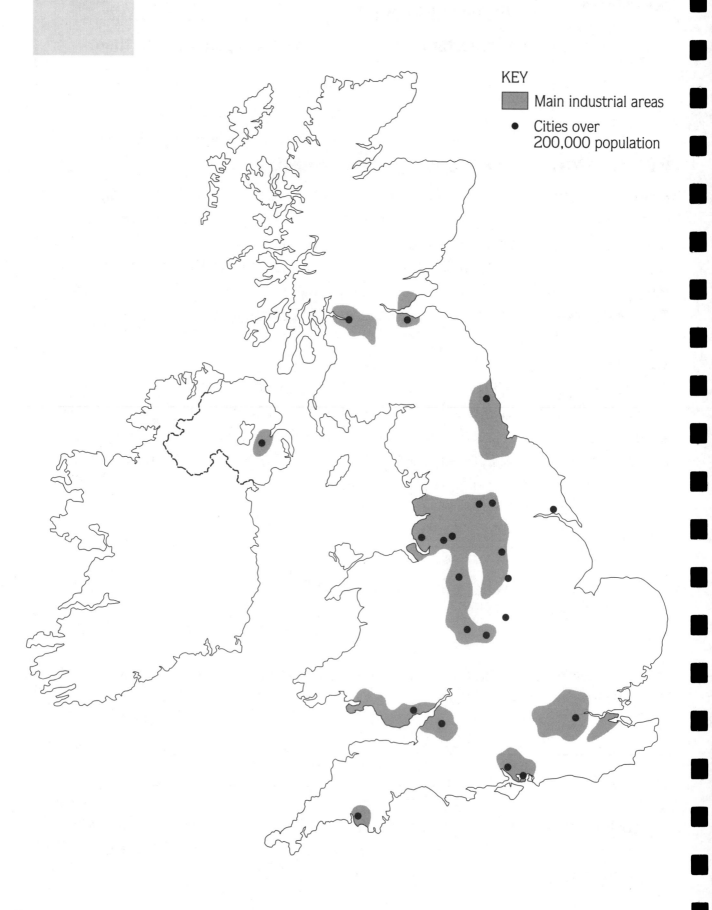

KEY

▨ Main industrial areas

● Cities over 200,000 population

26

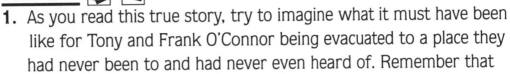

Your task

1. As you read this true story, try to imagine what it must have been like for Tony and Frank O'Connor being evacuated to a place they had never been to and had never even heard of. Remember that they came from a big city.

2. When you have finished reading the story, imagine you are either Farmer Davies or Mrs Davies, the two people who took the boys in. Rewrite the story from their point of view.

The story of the soggy sandwiches

Tony and Frank O'Connor were just two of the 1.5 million people who were evacuated during September 1939. They were the lucky ones. They were able to stay together. They were also with their friends since most of the children from their school were sent to a place called Dyserth in North Wales. The evening they arrived had been really terrible. Everyone stood around in a draughty church hall whilst a lady called out their names from a long list.

Then some people came in. The women went round examining the boys' hands and faces and looking at their clothes. The men were more interested in seeing how tall and strong-looking they were. Tony and Frank obviously looked reasonably fit because they were some of the first to be chosen. A Mr and Mrs Davies, who were sheep farmers, called them over.

'You two are brothers we hear,' said Mrs Davies. She had a sing-song Welsh accent. 'Well, you look clean enough. We need two strong lads to help on the farm. I suppose you'll do!'

With that, the two boys were led away.

The farmhouse where they were staying wasn't too bad. At least they were in the same bedroom, even though it was a tiny room in the attic. The real problem was food. There just wasn't enough of it. Mrs Davies was particularly mean. She almost seemed to take pleasure in doling out huge helpings of stew to her husband and herself and then putting a tiny portion on the boys' plates.

'I'm sure this is more than you'd get at home' she would say.

One day Tony and Frank were playing in the yard. Mrs Davies called them inside. 'I'm expecting a visit from the Welfare Officer,' she said, 'so smarten yourselves up and make sure you tell her how good we have been to you.'

'Good to us, my foot,' whispered Frank to his brother. 'Why, she half starves us!'

'Come on now,' said Tony. 'It's not that bad. We're just used to being spoiled by Mum and Kay and Joan.'

Frank wasn't convinced. He wandered into the kitchen to get some soap. There on the table was a huge plate of sandwiches.

'Now you just leave them alone,' said Mrs Davies. 'They're for the Welfare Officer when she comes.' She went upstairs to get a clean tablecloth. Frank was really cross. He went out to find Tony and told him all about it. 'The Welfare Officer will think that WE get sandwiches like this for tea,' he moaned. 'Well, I'll give her sandwiches to remember!' With that, Frank ran back into the kitchen. He picked up every single sandwich, spat inside each one, then put it back on the plate.

'So much for delicious sandwiches,' he smiled.

The afternoon wore on but there was no sign of the Welfare Officer. Then the telephone rang. A few minutes later Mrs Davies came outside. She was smiling.

'That was the Welfare Officer on the phone. She can't visit us this afternoon because one of the evacuees has run away, so she's dealing with the police. My goodness, it makes me realise how lucky I am having two such sensible boys as you. I know, as a treat, you must come inside and share all these sandwiches with me and Mr Davies. They're your favourite,' she said. 'Spam sandwiches.'

'Spam and spit you mean,' whispered Frank to himself. But he could do nothing about it. The two boys went inside. Tony didn't know what on earth was wrong with Frank. He was thrilled at the thought of extra sandwiches. Politely the two boys waited for Mrs Davies to take the first sandwich. Frank looked rather pale. She took a bite and then her face just crumpled up.

'Who on earth?' she shouted. Tony looked around. Where was Frank?

~~~~~~

☞ Use this sheet to rewrite the story from Farmer Davies' or Mrs Davies' point of view.

THE BOYS
FROM LIVERPOOL

_____

_____

_____

_____

_____

_____

_____

_____

_____

_____

_____

_____

_____

_____

_____

27

You will need
- pen or pencil

◆ **HISTORY DICTIONARY**

The important words	My explanation of them
Blitz	_____
	_____

The Blitz begins

For nearly twelve months after war had been declared on Germany, the people living in the big industrial cities waited for the bombs to be dropped. But nothing happened. Some families that had been evacuated began to move back home. Others became careless about blackouts or forgot to carry their gas masks around with them.

The O'Connors were sensible, however. Tony and Frank stayed in North Wales and their parents drove to visit them once every two or three weeks. It had taken several boxes of chocolate biscuits to calm Mrs Davies down after the spitting incident. But by August 1940, even she could see the funny side of it.

On 7 September 1940, at 4.36 pm, the air-raid sirens started in London. A few minutes later, the East End of London was being showered with bombs. For twelve solid hours the bombs dropped. During this time, 436 people were killed and 1600 severely injured. The photograph above shows a scene in London during the Blitz.

Over the next eight weeks, the Germans bombed London nearly every night. Then they bombed Glasgow, Coventry and Liverpool. By May 1941, when the **Blitz** ended, one and a half million people in London had been made homeless. Across the country, 43,000 people had been killed.

Your task

Read Source 1 on page 2. Then read the four statements about the First-aid Wardens who were normally the first people on the scene after a bomb had exploded.

1. Decide which words and sentences from Source 1 back up each statement.
2. Record them underneath the correct statement.

THE TWENTIETH-CENTURY WORLD SUPPORT MATERIALS © JOHN MURRAY

SOURCE 1 A first-hand account of the Blitz by a First-aid Warden, 14 September 1940

The church was a popular shelter. People felt that nowhere would they be safer than under the protection of the Church – so it was full when the bomb fell.

The bomb had burst into the middle of the shelterers, mostly women and small children. The scene resembled a massacre with bodies, limbs, blood and flesh mingled with little hats, coats and shoes. The people were literally blown to pieces. The work of the ARP (first aiders) services was magnificent – by nine o'clock all the casualties were out.

After a heavy raid there was the task of piecing the bodies together in preparation for burial. The stench was the worst thing about it – that, and having to realise that these frightful pieces of flesh had once been living breathing people. There were always odd limbs which did not fit, and there were too many legs. Unless we kept a very firm grip on ourselves, nausea was inevitable.

Normally, the First-aid Wardens came across really horrible sights. evidence:	The First-aid Wardens found it difficult not to become too emotional. evidence:
The First-aid Wardens were very organised and knew exactly what to do. evidence:	The First-aid Wardens were extremely brave. evidence:

28

You will need

- pen or pencil

Keeping up morale

The Germans knew exactly what they were doing when they bombed British cities. They wanted to destroy people's morale and make them surrender. The British airforce was doing the same to the big German cities.

SOURCE 1 King and Queen visit people sheltering in the London Underground

The government made sure that nothing really dreadful was ever printed in the newspapers. Reporters were not allowed to show pictures of bombed houses or dead bodies. Instead, they had to report that everyone was carrying on as normal and working together!

Your task

Here are four different sources. They each tell you a little bit about the Blitz. You can also find all the sources on pages 166–167 of *Peace & War*.

1. Which two sources would the government have allowed to be printed in British newspapers?
2. Explain why you have chosen these sources.

SOURCE 3 Injured man talking to civil defence worker in the ruins of his home, November 1940

SOURCE 2 A report from Coventry after a heavy air raid, 1940

There were more open signs of hysteria and terror than observed in the previous two months. The overwhelming feeling on Friday was the feeling of utter helplessness. The tremendous impact of the previous night had left many people speechless. On Friday evening [15 November], there were several signs of suppressed panic as darkness approached.

SOURCE 4 Letter from Humphrey Jennings to his wife, October 1940

What warmth – what courage! What determination. People singing in public shelters. WVS [Women's Voluntary Service] girls serving hot drinks to firefighters during raids. Everyone secretly delighted with the privilege of holding up Hitler. Certain of beating him.

 Why would the government try to 'censor' some of these sources? Do you think they were right to do this?

29

You will need

- pen or pencil

Women at work

As far as women were concerned, the Second World War was a repeat of what had happened to them in the First World War. Suddenly they were in great demand. Jobs which were once done only by men were soon being done just as well by women.

Kay and Joan O'Connor found themselves doing different jobs too. Joan was still at school, but every evening when she got home, she went out with her father collecting insurance money and helping people who had lost their belongings in the Blitz. Kay joined the Women's Auxiliary Services and spent most of the War as a nurse, looking after wounded soldiers.

Your task

Examine Sources 1–6. You can also find these sources on pages 168–169 of *Peace & War*.

1. Make a list of all the jobs that women did during the War.
2. What do you think a woman would have said about this sort of work in 1935? What do you think she would have said in 1945 when the War was over? Write your answers in the correct speech bubbles on page 3.

SOURCE 1 An advertisement in a women's magazine during the War

SOURCE 2 Women workers in a munitions factory

SOURCE 3 From a speech by Clement Atlee, Deputy Prime Minister, in September 1942

The work the women are performing in munitions [weapons] factories has to be seen to be believed. Precision engineering jobs which a few years ago would have made a skilled turner's hair stand on end are performed with dead accuracy by girls who have had no industrial experience.

SOURCE 5 Forty years after the War one woman remembered her work in the Land Army

The people were very resentful in the country, they didn't make it easy for you, we weren't really welcome. All we had in the Land Army digs [lodgings] were sausages, every day for nine months. The landlady used to cook them in water, they were horrible.

I was sent to a farm in Essex. There were four of us in a gang assigned to an old steam tractor with a threshing machine behind. Two of us switched the switch over and hooked the sacks on, the others threw the corn in the bin. It was very hard work. We had to go where the tackle was and sometimes we biked eight miles or so before beginning. Later I planted potatoes.

SOURCE 4 Members of the Women's Land Army at work. In 1939 the Women's Land Army, which had been set up during the First World War, was started up again. Even before conscription to war work was introduced in 1941, 30,000 women had volunteered for it

SOURCE 6 Some women joined the Air Transport Auxiliary and flew newly built planes to air bases. This photograph shows an ATA pilot who has just delivered a Wellington bomber

What I felt about women working in 1935

Jobs that women did in the War

_____

_____

_____

_____

_____

_____

_____

What I felt about women working in 1945

30

You will need

- counters
- a dice
- game board
- clothing chance cards
- food chance cards
- clothing coupon points
- food token points

◆ **HISTORY DICTIONARY**

The important words	My explanation of them
rationing	_____
	_____

Rationing

On 8 January 1940, six months after the War had begun, the government decided to introduce food **rationing**. The following year, in June 1941, the government introduced clothes rationing. This was necessary because a great deal of the food and clothing that people ate and wore came from abroad. The Germans were bombing British ships and planes so the government couldn't rely on getting supplies from abroad.

Another problem was the ships themselves. Many were needed to transport soldiers and weapons rather than food and clothing. So the government tried to encourage people to grow their own food and to 'make do and mend' as much as possible with clothing.

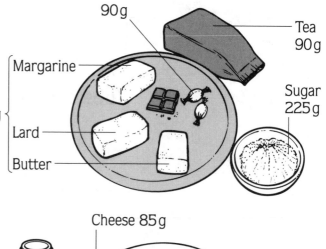

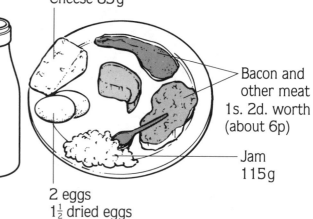

Typical weekly food rations per person. Bread was never rationed, nor were fruit, vegetables, fish or offal (parts of the animal such as the heart, liver and tongue).

Most people welcomed rationing because it was fair. Before it was introduced, rich people could get whatever they wanted, if they paid enough money, but poorer people often didn't have enough to eat.

But rationing didn't solve all the problems. Many people 'found ways round it'. A few people would use their savings to buy 'black market' food tokens or clothing coupons. This was dangerous and if people were caught they could get into serious trouble. It was also unfair because it meant that some goods, such as nylon stockings for instance, became very scarce. In times of war, there are always people who will make a profit out of someone else's bad luck.

Usually, however, the 'wheeling and dealing' was just careful management. Perhaps extra food was wanted for a special occasion like a birthday. If this was the case, people might trade in their clothing coupons for extra food points or they would be very careful in the weeks leading up to the birthday and use fewer food points than they were allowed.

New clothes might be needed for a wedding. Some families grew vegetables in their gardens. Perhaps they would sell these more cheaply than in the shops and be given some unwanted clothing coupons in return? If they were good at needlework, they could make dresses and coats out of old sheets and bedspreads. This would leave them enough clothing coupons to buy a smart new outfit. People found many ways round the new rules without breaking the law and still spending their rations wisely.

Your task

1. Read Sources 1–3 below.
2. Underline all the evidence in the sources which shows that people in wartime Britain were very resourceful.

SOURCE 1 From a school history book

People used all sorts of things to replace food that vanished. Nettles tasted like spinach when boiled and could be dried for tea. Sugar and sweets were rare. It was illegal to ice cakes, so people hired cardboard wedding cakes for show. Women made jam and cakes with carrots.

SOURCE 2 Helen Forrester, *Lime Street at Two*

Over several lunches, the girls in the office discussed the situation and agreed that stockings were out. We shaved our legs and went bare legged. Our skin looked horribly white, and all wrong with heavy shoes. So we experimented with painting the part that showed. One girl swore by gravy browning, and even went as far as drawing a careful line up the back of her legs with her eyebrow pencil, to give a resemblance of a stocking seam.

SOURCE 3 Juliet Gardiner, *The People's War*

Everything that could be was turned into something else: a coat from a candlewick bedspread, a blouse from dusters, a skirt from blackout material, a dress from a sheet or tablecloth, whilst surplus service blankets were seized upon and transformed into winter coats and dressing gowns.

3. What do you think the slogan on this government poster meant?

This slogan meant _____

_____

_____

_____

_____

Your task
You should be in groups of four for this task.

It is September 1941. Frank, Tony, Kay and Joan O'Connor are all saving up for two special events. Their father James will be 60 in six months. They want to give him a surprise birthday party with all his favourite food. Their cousin Alma is going to get married on Christmas Eve. They want smart new outfits for the wedding. Everyone is determined to make sacrifices. Everyone is sure they will be able to save up their coupons and tokens.

Who will be able to save up the most clothing coupons and food tokens for the two special occasions?

1. Decide who will be Frank, Tony, Kay and Joan.
2. Each person starts with 20 clothing coupon points and 20 food token points. Leave the rest of the clothing coupons and food tokens in their boxes.
3. Place the clothing and food chance cards on the board.
4. Put all your counters on the start box.
5. Take it in turns to throw the dice.
6. If you land on a shaded square, pick up a card from the correct pile.
7. Follow the instructions on the card which will tell you how many clothing and food points you will win or lose.
8. Replace the card at the bottom of the pile.
9. When everyone has been around the game board twice, count up all the points on your clothing coupons and food tokens.

Who will be able to provide the most food for James' party?

Who will have the smartest outfit for Alma's wedding?

30

Resource Sheet 1

Game board

Enlarge to A3 size. Copy this on to card, one per group.

Pick up a CLOTHING card		Pick up a FOOD card		Pick up a CLOTHING card		START — Collect 20 Food token points and 20 Clothing coupon points

Food chance cards

Replace used cards at the bottom of the pile

Pick up a FOOD card

Pick up a FOOD card

Pick up a FOOD card — Pick up a CLOTHING card

Pick up a FOOD card

Pick up a CLOTHING card

Clothing chance cards

Replace used cards at the bottom of the pile

Pick up a FOOD card

| Pick up a CLOTHING card | | Pick up a FOOD card | | Pick up a CLOTHING card | | Pick up a CLOTHING card | Pick up a FOOD card |

Clothing chance cards

Copy on to coloured paper or card, one set per game board.

You bought six pairs of stockings on the black market. When you got them home, you found that each pair was full of holes. It has really taught you a lesson!
Lose 10 clothing coupon points

You have grown out of your new blazer so quickly that it is hardly worn at all. You swap it with Mrs Taylor in return for extra clothing coupons.
Collect 8 clothing coupon points

You find an old candlewick bedspread in the cupboard. You turn it into a snug coat to wear to work. This means you don't have to buy a new winter coat.
Collect 10 clothing coupon points

You caught the pocket of your new suit on the corner of the table. The jacket is torn to shreds. You have to buy a new jacket to go to work in.
Lose 6 clothing coupon points

You find some unused knitting wool and make a beautiful set of baby clothes for Mrs Jackson's new baby. She gives you two clothing coupons as a thank-you gift.
Collect 2 clothing coupon points

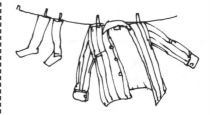

You hang out two pairs of socks and a shirt to dry. Someone comes along and steals them. You are forced to go out and buy some new ones.
Lose 6 clothing coupon points

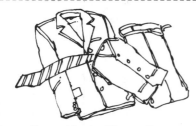

Great Uncle Albert dies peacefully in his sleep. His wife lets you have one of his old suits and two or three ties. This saves you a lot of coupons.
Collect 6 clothing coupon points

You decide to do without a new pair of shoes this year. You have your old pair soled and heeled.
Collect 8 clothing coupon points

It is a very warm September. You have grown out of your summer clothes but are so hot that you have to buy a new short sleeved shirt.
Lose 4 clothing coupon points

Copy on to coloured paper or card, one set per game board.

Your friend's house, where you have been staying, suffers a direct hit in the Blitz. You lose every shred of clothing apart from those you are wearing. You have to replace some of them.
Lose 20 clothing coupon points

The local draper has some old pre-war stock to get rid of. He lets you buy it cheaply. This includes several sets of underwear. It saves you a few coupons.
Collect 2 clothing coupon points

You unravel an old jumper and manage to knit enough warm balaclavas for the whole family. You don't have to spend any coupons on hats.
Collect 2 clothing coupon points

A so-called friend offers you a sweater. He says he bought it legally but has grown out of it. You wear it to a party and find out that it was stolen from the nearby department store. You daren't wear it again.
Lose 4 clothing coupon points

The street next to yours was bombed. The bomb fractured a water main which flooded all the houses in your area. You had a pile of clothes in a washing basket. They were all ruined.
Lose 8 clothing coupon points

You get a friend to make a smart new dress out of a pair of curtains for your aunt to wear at her 50th birthday party. She is so pleased with it that she gives you some of her clothing coupons.
Collect 6 clothing coupon points

Mrs Adams from down the road has lost two sons who were killed at Dunkirk. She offers you their old school uniforms. It is a very sad time for her, but she is pleased to be able to help. This saves you a lot of coupons.
Collect 8 clothing coupon points

A German bomber was shot down in the fields nearby. The pilot parachuted to safety. He was captured, but mysteriously his parachute was never found. Everyone in your neighbourhood, including you, now has beautiful silk underwear! This saves you some coupons of course.
Collect 4 clothing coupon points

You save your clothing coupons for three months because you want to buy a cheap pair of trousers that are being advertised in a nearby shop. By the time you have saved up enough, all the trousers have gone. You are forced to buy a really expensive pair.
Lose 4 clothing coupon points

Food chance cards

Copy on to coloured paper or card, one set per game board.

You saved all your sweet rations for six weeks. It is really difficult to do this because the sweets are so tempting. But you manage. They will look great on the table at James' party. The shopkeeper has promised you two extra weeks' ration if you keep it up!
Collect 4 food token points

You sell your favourite set of *Beano* comics to the boy who lives down the street. He gives you his weekly sweets ration in return.
Collect 2 food token points

James doesn't like cheese. You ask him for his weekly cheese rations, saying that it is to help you grow strong teeth and gums. Instead, you sell them and buy him a new crystal radio set with the money. The man next door is so impressed with you that he gives you his own cheese rations!
Collect 4 food token points

You go without sugar in your tea for two months. The savings you make will allow you to bake a lovely carrot cake for James' birthday.
Collect 4 food token points

You sell your meat ration to the couple next door and make do with vegetable soups and fish. They give you some fresh eggs which you can hoard.
Collect 6 food token points

You bake half a dozen extra loaves that smell really beautiful. A neighbour passing by asks if she could have them in return for some of her sugar points.
Collect 4 food token points

Your friend's brother gets ten extra food points a week because he is a manual labourer. He was off sick for a few days and sold his points to you in return for a set of his favourite detective novels.
Collect 10 food token points

You deliberately cultivate a bed of nettles in your garden. Eventually you will be able to boil them for spinach or dry the leaves to make tea. This will leave you with some extra money to buy a few food points.
Collect 2 food token points

You drain all the fish oil from the week's mackerel meal. The following week you spread this on your toast rather than butter. You save the butter points for James' birthday party.
Collect 4 food token points

Your refrigerator breaks down. The meat and butter goes rancid. You are forced to use some of the extra tokens you have saved in order to prepare a proper Sunday dinner.
Lose 6 food token points

Your mother Elizabeth gets bronchitis. The whole family has to pool its sugar rations to make soothing drinks for her throat.
Lose 4 food token points

You can't resist taking an extra piece of fruit cake which Elizabeth had spent hours baking. When she finds out, you have to repay some of your sweets points.
Lose 2 food token points

A shipment of fresh meat and eggs which was supposed to arrive at the Albert Dock fails to turn up. Everyone's rations are cut for four weeks. You are forced to trade in some spare food points for cash, so that you can buy fish instead.
Lose 8 food token points

You use up all the stocks of powdered egg trying to make an omelette. It is so revolting that you throw it away without eating any of it. Rashly you go out and buy some ham instead.
Lose 6 food token points

The bombed-out houses have created a health hazard. Rats are roaming the streets. You wake up one morning to find a dead rat floating on the top of the milk pail. You have to throw the milk away and buy some more.
Lose 4 food token points

Your best friend has got a magazine with all the latest fashions. You are dying to see it so that you can decide what to wear for Alma's wedding. She lets you have it for some sweets points.
Lose 4 food token points

Your elder brothers, James and Louis, come over from Seacombe to visit. Elizabeth persuades everyone to let her have some of the extra points they have saved so that she can give James and Louis a special tea.
Lose 4 food token points

The O'Hanlon family down the road has been made homeless in the latest bombing raid. There are six children. You invite them to stay at 10 Jubilee Avenue for two weeks until the council can rehouse them. They have lost their ration books, so you share everything out equally. All your extra points are lost.
Lose 10 food token points

Clothing coupon points

Copy these on to card and reproduce as many as are necessary for the game. Cut each coupon out and store in a box.

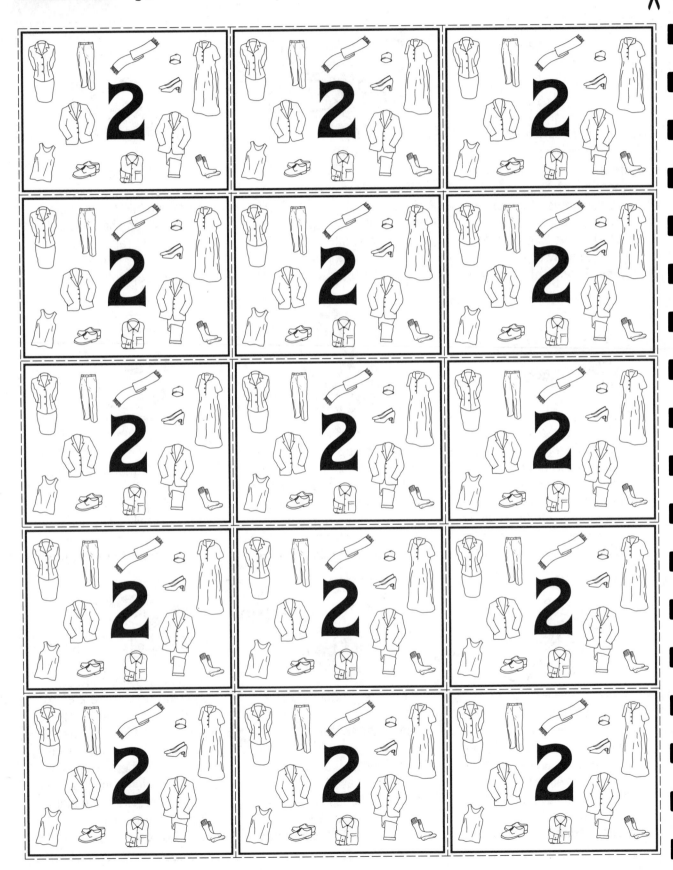

THE TWENTIETH-CENTURY WORLD SUPPORT MATERIALS © JOHN MURRAY

Food token points

Copy these on to card and reproduce as many as are necessary for the game. Cut each token out and store in a box.

There are five pages to this task

~~~~~~

You will need

- pen or pencil

◆ **HISTORY DICTIONARY**

The important words	My explanation of them
Allies	_____
civilians	_____
occupation	_____
surrendered	_____

How did people in Britain and Germany feel about the War?

On 3 September 1939, Britain and France declared war on Germany. The nations that were on Britain's side were called the **Allies** and the two main countries that fought against the Allies were Germany and Japan. Italy also fought on Germany's side for four years.

The War lasted for six years. During those years about twenty million soldiers died, ten million **civilians** were killed and over six million Jews were murdered. There was fighting all over the world, but most of the battles were in Europe or Asia. People from nearly every single nation in the world got caught up in the fighting. Many countries were under **occupation** by enemy soldiers. The Allies eventually won the War.

In May 1945, Germany **surrendered** and Adolf Hitler committed suicide. Three months later, in August 1945, the Americans (who had joined the Allies in 1941) dropped two atom bombs on Japan. The Japanese surrendered.

Your task 📝 📖

On pages 2–5 there is a timeline of some of the main events of the Second World War.
Alongside each event are two brief descriptions of it.
They are imaginary newspaper descriptions. This means that they are interpretations of what might have really been written.

Which description might have been printed by a German newspaper and which by a British newspaper? Put a G for German or B for British in the box next to each description.

~~~~~~

The events of the Second World War

Decide which description would have been printed in a German newspaper and which in a British newspaper. Now write the letter G or B in the box by each description. Do this for pages 3–5 too.

1939 **September** Germany invades Poland. Britain and France declare war on Germany	Our great nation is being threatened by the old enemy Britain. All we have done is try to protect our German borders.		This time Germany has gone too far. Poland must be supported. We made a treaty with Poland. Adolf Hitler must be stopped.	
1940 **10 May** Germany invades Holland 	Yet again we have shown that Germany is the greatest nation. Holland is on our borders. We have invaded it for our own protection.		Holland has been a good friend to Britain for centuries. We have always traded in wool and cloth. It is one of our closest neighbours across the North Sea. We must drive Hitler out of Holland.	
1940 **27 May** Britain evacuates army from Dunkirk (a beach in France) 	All night and all day the undefeated British soldiers have come back in glory. They were collected by brave civilians in fishing boats, rowing boats, ships and steamers. This is a great victory for British team spirit and morale.		We cornered the British and French armies on the beach at Dunkirk. Our brave fighter pilots were able to destroy thousands of them. A raggedy fleet of ancient boats and ships managed to rescue those cowards who had hidden down on the beaches.	
1940 **22 June** France signs a peace agreement with Germany. German soldiers occupy France 	Ha! Now we have taken our revenge on France. Millions of Germans will remember how the French insisted that we pay huge fines after the First World War. Our children starved. Our men had no work. But did the French care? No! Revenge is sweet.		So France has fallen to the German war machine. Have no fear, brave French men and women of the Resistance. We remember how bravely you fought in the First World War. We will come to your rescue.	

1940 **July–October** Battle of Britain. British and German planes fight the war in the air 	They have more fighter planes and bombers than us. They have more trained pilots. But we have used brilliant tactics. We aimed at their bombers. We forced Germany to call off its plans for invasion.	We destroyed hundreds and hundreds of fighter planes. Then we realised that we could bomb the factories where the planes were being made. Our plans were the cleverest.
1941 **June** Germany invades the USSR (Russia) 	Now that we have Poland, we must protect ourselves from the Russian Communists. They are evil people who threaten our freedom. All good Germans must fight the threat of Communism.	The Russians need our help. We know they are all Communists and that all decent people hate Communism, but the Nazis are even more evil than the Communists. Anyway, we need Russian soldiers and Russian weapons.
1941 **December** Japan attacks the US naval base at Pearl Harbor. The USA declares war on Japan. Germany and Italy declare war on the USA 	During the First World War, the USA joined with Britain and France to fight against us. That is why we lost. Never again. This time, we will declare war on them. They are at war with Japan now. What a great time for Germany and Italy to declare war on them!	The Americans are our oldest friends. We relied on them in the First World War. Many of our ancestors emigrated to America. We must join forces. They will help us in Europe against the Germans and Italians. We will help them in the Pacific against the Japanese.
1942 **May–November** The Allies are beginning to win battles in Africa, Asia, the Pacific and the USSR 	Just as we predicted, the Germans are losing their touch. The great armies of Britain, the USA and the USSR, are winning all over the world. Mark our words. The days of German victories are over!	Our brave soldiers continue to bring honour to their country. They fight in Russia, Africa and Asia. They are fearless and strong. They fight to protect all the lands which now belong to Germany, such as France, Holland, Poland and Czechoslovakia.

~~~~~~

1943 **July–September** The Germans are losing ground in the USSR. Italy surrenders to the Allies 	Our great leader, Adolf Hitler, sees how much his people need him. He has unselfishly decided to leave Russia so that his soldiers can visit their loved ones at home. What a great and good leader we have!	Hitler is on the run. The Russian army is all set for a brilliant victory. Even better news comes from Italy where Mussolini has been driven from power. Now the Italians are on our side. Hitler does not stand a chance.
1944 **6 June D-Day** The Allied army invades France and begins its long march towards Germany 	You would not believe the great news about the War. Our armies have landed safely in France. We are marching towards Paris. The Germans are on the run. Soon the War will be over.	Have no fear, people of Germany. Our soldiers are brave and true. They are leaving France to join the troops returning from the USSR. When THIS great army meets, no one will be able to enter Germany. Our Fatherland is safe.
1945 **February** The Allied army invades Germany, reaching Berlin in April 	HUNS ON THE RUN! Jerry is driven back into his lair. Our brave soldiers have done it again. Long live freedom.	16 February 1945 All files which deal with anti-Jewish activities are to be destroyed.
1945 **8 May** Germany surrenders. Hitler commits suicide 	The War is now over. Germany has surrendered. Millions of our people have died. Hitler, our leader, is dead. We must pray that the Allies don't make us pay as dearly for the War as they did in 1918. We must hope for mercy from our enemies.	The War is now over. Germany has surrendered. Millions of our people have died. Hitler, the evil Führer, is dead. We must show mercy to the German people. They have suffered as much as us. We will make them pay for what they have done, but we must be fair.

1945 **6 August** First atom bomb dropped on Japanese city of Hiroshima 	Reports are coming in of a huge bomb which the Americans have dropped in Japan. Some people say that hundreds of thousands of human beings have just melted in the heat. The Allies have no concern for ordinary civilians. Just look what they did to our beautiful city of Dresden in Germany.	What wonderful news. The Americans have dropped the first atom bomb on Japan. They have destroyed all the Japanese factories and war machines. Soon we will have won the war in the Pacific as well as the war in Europe. Soon all our soldiers will come home.
1945 **9 August** Second atom bomb dropped on Nagasaki 	I can hardly believe the news that has just come in. The Americans have dropped another atom bomb. They have destroyed the entire city of Nagasaki. When will all this horror stop?	This time the Japs really know we mean business! Mark my words, they will surrender soon. If they don't, our allies the Americans will blow the whole of Japan off this planet.
1945 **14 August** Japan surrenders. Second World War finally over 	ALLIED VICTORY IN JAPAN AS WELL AS EUROPE	ALLIED VICTORY IN JAPAN AS WELL AS EUROPE

 ■ **Do you think these interpretations of history help you understand how people felt at the time?**
■ **Are they as helpful as the real newspapers would have been?**

DEPTH STUDY 6

The Holocaust: what was it and why did it happen?

♦ **HISTORY DICTIONARY**

The important words	My explanation of them
Jew	
discrimination	
persecution	
concentration camp	
Holocaust	

One of the most terrible events of the Second World War was the murder by Hitler and the Nazis of millions of **Jews**. Hitler hated the Jews and blamed all Germany's problems on them. To start with, the Nazis simply discriminated against the Jews. But gradually **discrimination** became active **persecution**. Eventually, persecution turned into the most awful slaughter. Jews were sent to **concentration camps** where they were starved and gassed to death. This is known as the **Holocaust**. The Nazis also murdered thousands of gypsies, homosexuals, Russian prisoners of war, tramps and mentally-ill people.

This depth study examines why the Holocaust happened at all. It allows you to think about how you can prevent such an awful thing ever happening again.

32

You will need
- pen or pencil

♦ **HISTORY DICTIONARY**

The important words	My explanation of them
anti-Semitism	_____
	_____
Christians	_____
	_____
	_____
ghetto	_____
	_____
	_____

Was anti-Semitism common in Europe?

The growth of anti-Semitism in Europe

For nearly 2000 years, ever since Jesus Christ died, Jewish people have been blamed for his death. Some **Christians** (the followers of Christ) said that because some Jews had killed Christ, all the Jews were responsible for this crime. They said that the Jews deserved to suffer just like Christ had done.

Over the centuries, wherever Jewish people tried to settle, Christians have turned on them. They would attack innocent Jewish men, women and children. They would make cruel jokes about their clothes, their faces and their religion. Often, Jewish people would also be kicked, beaten or driven from their homes. A vicious rumour began that during the Passover (a Jewish festival), Jews killed Christian babies to make bread with their blood. There was no truth whatsoever in this rumour. At various times in the past Christians have murdered Jews for no other reason than that they were Jews. Jews were herded into buildings, locked inside and the buildings burnt down.

Often it was rulers such as kings or bishops who were happy to see the Jews being treated badly. This was because many Jews were bankers. At first, kings and bishops welcomed them because the Jews would lend them money to pay for armies or to build beautiful cathedrals. They would even encourage the Jews to live near their castles or palaces in Jewish quarters or **ghettos**. This was supposedly to protect the Jews from persecution.

But when the Jewish bankers asked for the money to be repaid, things would turn nasty. The kings or bishops either could not or did not want to pay the money they owed. So they would encourage ordinary people to persecute the Jews. To stir up trouble, they spread stories about the Jews being Christ-killers, or that they were scheming and greedy.

32

The ghettos became like prisons and Jews living there were constantly being attacked by gangs of thugs. Often these attacks ended in death and mutilation. People would become jealous of the homes Jews lived in, the jobs they had, any money they made and any talents they showed.

This behaviour is known as **anti-Semitism**. It still goes on today.

Over the centuries Jews have been presented as ugly, greedy, sly and, most dangerous of all, almost non-human.

Your task

On pages 3–5 are some examples of the ways Jews have been attacked over the past 2000 years.

1. Examine or read each source carefully.
2. Explain, in the space provided, how the Jews are being persecuted.
3. List the attacks in chronological order on the timeline below.

Timeline of Jewish persecution

AD 2nd Century   Jews driven out of Judaea (now called Israel) by the Romans

AD 1940–1945   Six million European Jews murdered by Hitler

SOURCE 1 Charles Dickens, *Oliver Twist*, 1837–39

... standing over them with a toasting fork in his hand was a very old, shrivelled Jew, whose villainous looking and repulsive face was obscured by a quantity of matted red hair.

SOURCE 2 A sculpture showing Jews living in Germany during the eleventh century. They were forced to wear cone-shaped hats to mark them from the rest of the population

SOURCE 3 William Shakespeare, *The Merchant of Venice*, 1590s

SHYLOCK [A Jew]:
Signior Antonio, many a time and oft
In the Rialto you have rated me
About my moneys and my usances . . .
You call me misbeliever, cut-throat dog,
And spit upon my Jewish gaberdine . . .

ANTONIO [A Christian]:
I am as like to call thee so again,
To spit on thee again, to spurn thee too.

SOURCE 4 From a Roman Catholic prayer book, 1961

Let us pray also for Jews: that our God and Lord would remove the veil from their hearts: hear our prayers, which we offer for the blindness of that people: that acknowledging the light of thy truth which is Christ, they may be rescued from their darkness.

SOURCE 5 Manuscript line drawing and decree issued by the Archbishop of Canterbury, Stephen Langton, in 1222

To prevent likewise the mixture of Jewish men and women with Christians of each sex, we charge that Jews of both sexes wear a linen cloth, two inches broad and four fingers long of a different colour from their own clothes, on their upper garment before their breast.

SOURCE 6 Adolf Hitler, *Mein Kampf*, 1924

On putting the probing knife into (a problem) I found, like a maggot in a rotting body, a little Jew, often blinded by the sudden light . . . Was there any such undertaking, any form of foulness . . . in which at least one Jew did not participate?

There are four pages to this task

◆ **HISTORY DICTIONARY**

The important words	My explanation of them
Aryan	_____
	_____
	_____
propaganda	_____
	_____
	_____

How did the Nazis stir up hatred of the Jews?

As you saw in Task 32, anti-Semitism had been going on in Europe for two thousand years. During the 1930s, this anti-Semitism began again in Germany. The man who stirred up the age-old hatred of the Jews was Adolf Hitler. He said that all Germans should belong to the **Aryan** race. The ideal German was white-skinned, fair-haired and blue eyed. Hitler wanted the men to be strong and healthy, and good fighters. He wanted women to stay at home and look after their blond, healthy children.

Your task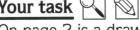

On page 2 is a drawing of a Nazi **propaganda** poster. It shows what Hitler wanted children to believe about Jewish people.

1. Label all the ways in which the poster tries to persuade German children that Jews were evil and useless.
2. Write a short paragraph explaining how the poster could have helped Hitler to increase anti-Semitism in Germany.

_____

_____

_____

_____

☞

Write your labels around this drawing of a Nazi propaganda poster.

THE TWENTIETH-CENTURY WORLD SUPPORT MATERIALS © JOHN MURRAY

☞

This is an outline drawing of another Nazi propaganda poster. You can find it on page 123 of *Peace & War*.

Your task ✎

1. Add labels around the drawing to show the features of Hitler's 'ideal' German family.
2. How would the poster help Hitler to increase anti-Semitism in Germany?

_____

_____

_____

■ **How did the people who drew these sources try to make ordinary men and women hate and despise the Jews?**

■ **Are there any other groups of people in society who suffer similar hatred?**

■ **Are there any children in your school who are picked on for what they look like or what they believe in?**

■ **Are these children being treated fairly?**

Your task

Read this poem. It was written by Martin Niemoller, a German pastor (vicar) who became a victim of the Nazis.

First they came for the Jews and I did
not speak out – because I was not a Jew.

Then they came for the communists and
I did not speak out – because I was not a communist.

Then they came for the trade unionists and I did
not speak out – because I was not a trade unionist.

Then they came for me –
and there was no one left
to speak out for me.

■ **What do you think Pastor Niemoller was trying to say?**

■ **What message is in this poem for people like you and me?**

34

You will need

- pen or pencil
- a set of cards showing anti-Semitic laws
- some sheets of A3 paper
- felt-tipped pens

♦ **HISTORY DICTIONARY**

The important words	My explanation of them
Nuremberg Laws	_____
synagogue	_____

What did Hitler do to the Jews in Germany during the 1930s?

Adolf Hitler became Chancellor of Germany in 1933. Soon he began to persecute the Jews. One Jewish man remembers how they all felt. 'Everybody shook. As kids of ten we shook.'

Hans Oppenheimer was extremely worried. He and his family were now living in Berlin, the capital of Germany. In 1935, Hitler passed a set of laws called the **Nuremberg Laws**. These meant that Jews lost all their rights as German citizens. This was just too much for Hans. He found another job in Holland and soon his wife, the two boys, both sets of grandparents and a new baby called Eve were living near Amsterdam in Holland.

Back in Germany, the persecution of the Jews gradually got worse. Slowly, but surely, all their rights and freedoms were taken away. (The photograph opposite shows Nazis pasting signs on a Jewish shop window to persuade people not to buy goods from them). On 9 November 1938, all over Germany, Nazi stormtroopers broke into and smashed up tens of thousands of  Jewish shops, homes and **synagogues** (the buildings where Jews hold their religious meetings). In many places, ordinary Germans joined in and helped the stormtroopers.

This night became known as *Kristallnacht* or the 'night of glass'.

Your task

You should work in pairs for this task.

1. Read Source 1 on page 2. It describes what happened to the Jews who were arrested on *Kristallnacht.*
2. Read the words on page 2. They describe the actions of the stormtroopers. With your partner, decide which word is the best description? Which word is the next best, etc?
3. Complete the statements on page 2.

> **SOURCE 1** Martin Gilbert, *The Holocaust*
>
> *At the gates the police were made to hand them over to an SS unit. The 62 Jews were then forced to run the gauntlet of spades, clubs and whips. The police, unable to bear their cries, turned their backs. As the Jews fell, they were beaten further. This 'orgy' of beating lasted half an hour. When it was over twelve were dead, their skulls smashed. The others were unconscious, some had their eyes knocked out, their faces flattened and shapeless.*

The SS men were:

- heartless
- evil
- cruel
- misguided
- sadistic
- triumphant

How would you describe the attitude of the German SS guards to the Jews they were beating up?

In our opinion, the word which best describes the attitudes of the German SS guards

is _____ . The reason we think this is _____

_____

_____

_____

We also think that _____ is a good word to describe them

because _____

_____

_____

We thought of several other words to describe what happened to the Jews after Kristallnacht. They are _____

_____

_____

34

A memorial in Berlin

In the early 1990s two German artists wanted to remind people of how German Jews had been treated in the 1930s and 1940s. They lived in an area of Berlin where many Jews had lived in the 1930s and 1940s. All around the area they put up 80 metal signs attached to lamp posts. On one side of each sign was a simple drawing of an everyday object. On the other, without any comment at all, was a law relating to that object.

In the task below you will use 32 of these lamp-post signs to see how the persecution of German Jews increased during the 1930s and 1940s.

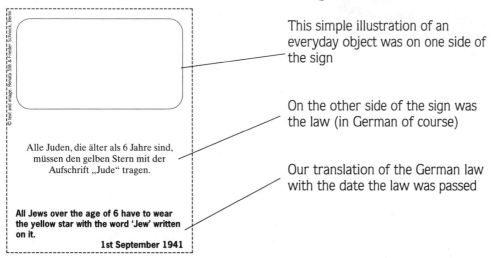

This simple illustration of an everyday object was on one side of the sign

On the other side of the sign was the law (in German of course)

Our translation of the German law with the date the law was passed

Alle Juden, die älter als 6 Jahre sind, müssen den gelben Stern mit der Aufschrift „Jude" tragen.

All Jews over the age of 6 have to wear the yellow star with the word 'Jew' written on it.
1st September 1941

Your task

Work in groups. You will need a set of cards from your teacher, several large sheets of plain paper and some felt-tipped pens to write with.

Each card has a date, picture and description of some of the laws Hitler made against the Jews.

1. Put your cards in chronological order.
2. Decide which law would most hurt: a) an adult b) a child.
3. Copy the law down on your sheet of paper.
4. Write underneath it WHY your group thinks it is so hurtful.
5. Now do the same with:
   ■ the law which your group thinks was the most humiliating
   ■ the law which your group thinks would have made the Jews most angry and frightened.
6. Make a list on your sheet of paper of all the reasons you can think of why the Jews in Germany were forced to accept these rules.
   Think about: ■ the violence of the Nazi stormtroopers
   ■ the attitudes of ordinary Germans to the Jews
   ■ the way each law was gradually imposed on the Jews
   ■ who would have benefited most from these laws.

Nazi laws against the Jews

Copy for each pupil. Cut out the four
cards along the dashed lines.

© text and image: Renata Stih & Frieder Schnock, Berlin

Juden dürfen kein Einzelhandels-
oder Versandgeschäft mehr
betreiben.

**Jews are banned from conducting a retail
or wholesale business.**
12th November 1938

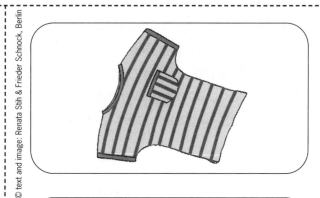

© text and image: Renata Stih & Frieder Schnock, Berlin

Alle Juden, die älter als 6 Jahre sind,
müssen den gelben Stern mit der
Aufschrift „Jude" tragen.

**All Jews over the age of 6 have to wear
the yellow star with the word 'Jew' written
on it.**
1st September 1941

© text and image: Renata Stih & Frieder Schnock, Berlin

Telefonanschlüsse von Juden
werden von der Post gekündigt.
Benutzungsverbot öffentlicher
Fernsprecher.

**Jews are to have their telephones
disconnected by the post office.**
29th July 1940
The use of public telephones is prohibited.
21st December 1941

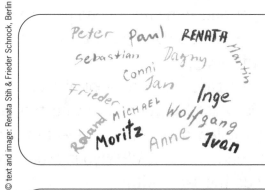

© text and image: Renata Stih & Frieder Schnock, Berlin

Juden müssen den Namen „Israel"
Jüdinnen den Namen „Sara" als
zusätzlichen Vornamen führen.

**Male Jews must add the name 'Israel' and
female Jews the name 'Sara' to their first
names.**
17th August 1938

Copy for each pupil. Cut out the four
cards along the dashed lines.

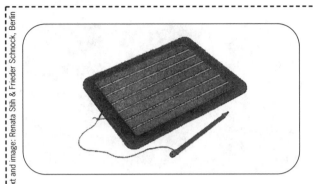

© text and image: Renata Stih & Frieder Schnock, Berlin

Jüdische Kinder dürfen keine
öffentlichen Schulen mehr
besuchen.
Verbot jeglichen Schulbesuchs.

**Jewish children are no longer allowed to
attend state schools.   15th November 1938
All schools closed to Jewish children.
20th June 1942**

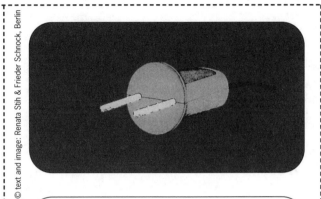

© text and image: Renata Stih & Frieder Schnock, Berlin

Juden müssen ihre elektrischen und
optischen Geräte, Fahrräder,
Schreibmaschinen und Schallplatten
abliefern.

**Jews must hand over their electrical and
optical equipment, bicycles, typewriters
and records.
29th January 1936**

© text and image: Renata Stih & Frieder Schnock, Berlin

Bei großem Andrang dürfen Juden
die öffentlichen Verkehrsmittel
nicht benutzen.
Sie dürfen Sitzplätze nur
einnehmen, wenn andere Reisende
nicht mehr stehen.

**During rush hour Jews are not permitted to
use public transport. They are only allowed
to occupy a seat if no other passengers
are standing.   18th September 1941**

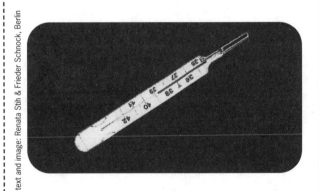

© text and image: Renata Stih & Frieder Schnock, Berlin

Jüdische Ärzte dürfen nicht mehr
praktizieren.

**Jewish doctors are not allowed to
practise any more.
25th July 1938**

Copy for each pupil. Cut out the four cards along the dashed lines.

© text and image: Renata Stih & Frieder Schnock, Berlin

Juden erhalten keine Kleiderkarten mehr.
Ablieferungszwang für Pelze und Wollsachen.

Jews are no longer to receive ration cards for clothes. January 1940
They are forced to hand over furs and woollen clothing. January 1942

© text and image: Renata Stih & Frieder Schnock, Berlin

Vererbungslehre und Rassenkunde werden an allen Schulen als Prüfungsgebiete eingeführt.

Genetic heredity and Race are to be introduced in all schools as part of the examination syllabus.
13th September 1933

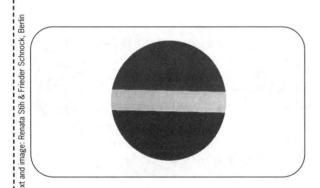

© text and image: Renata Stih & Frieder Schnock, Berlin

Bestimmte Bereiche der Stadt Berlin dürfen Juden nicht mehr betreten.

Jews are banned from certain districts in the city of Berlin.
3rd December 1938

© text and image: Renata Stih & Frieder Schnock, Berlin

Juden dürfen allgemeine Leih-büchereien nicht benutzen.
Juden dürfen keine Bücher mehr kaufen.

Jews are not allowed to use public libraries.
2nd August 1941
Jews are no longer allowed to buy books.
9th October 1942

Copy for each pupil. Cut out the four cards along the dashed lines.

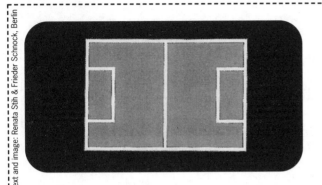

© text and image: Renata Stih & Frieder Schnock, Berlin

Juden werden aus Sport- und Turnvereinen ausgeschlossen.

Jews are excluded from sport and gymnastics clubs.

25th April 1933

© text and image: Renata Stih & Frieder Schnock, Berlin

Reisepässe von Juden müssen mit einem „J" gestempelt werden. Pässe von Juden, deren Ausreise unerwünscht ist, sind zu beschlagnahmen.

Jewish passports have to be stamped with a 'J'. Passports of Jews whose emigration is undesirable are to be confiscated.

5th October 1938

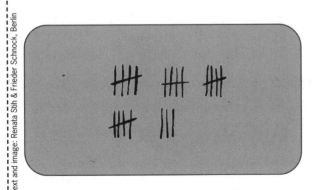

© text and image: Renata Stih & Frieder Schnock, Berlin

Jüdische Anwälte und Notare dürfen in Zukunft nicht in Rechtsangelegenheiten der Stadt Berlin tätig sein. Jüdische Richter werden beurlaubt.

Jewish lawyers and notaries are in future not allowed to conduct legal affairs for the city of Berlin. **18th March 1933**
Jewish judges are suspended from office.
31st March 1933

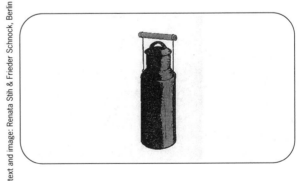

© text and image: Renata Stih & Frieder Schnock, Berlin

Juden erhalten keine Eier mehr. Keine Frischmilch für Juden.

Jews are no longer to receive eggs.
22nd June 1942
No fresh milk for Jews.
10th July 1942

Copy for each pupil. Cut out the four cards along the dashed lines.

© text and image: Renata Stih & Frieder Schnock, Berlin

Sämtliche Berliner Bezirksämter sind angewiesen, jüdische Lehrkräfte an den Städtischen Schulen sofort zu beurlauben.

All Berlin district councils are to relieve Jewish teachers in municipal schools of their office, with immediate effect.
1st April 1933

© text and image: Renata Stih & Frieder Schnock, Berlin

Akten, deren Gegenstand anti-jüdische Tätigkeiten sind, sind zu vernichten.

Files which deal with anti-Jewish activities are to be destroyed.
16th February 1945

© text and image: Renata Stih & Frieder Schnock, Berlin

Juden dürfen keine Haustiere mehr halten.

Jews are no longer allowed to keep pets.
15th May 1942

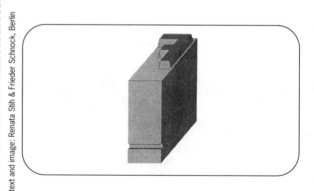

© text and image: Renata Stih & Frieder Schnock, Berlin

Jüdische Verlage und Buchhandlungen sind bis zum Jahresende aufzulösen.

Jewish publishing houses and bookshops are to be closed down by the end of the year.
December 1938

Copy for each pupil. Cut out the four cards along the dashed lines.

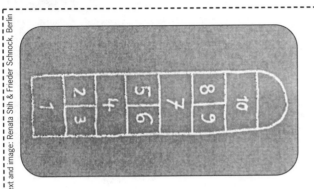

© text and image: Renata Stih & Frieder Schnock, Berlin

Arischen und nichtarischen Kindern wird das Spielen miteinander untersagt.

Aryan and non-Aryan children are forbidden to play together.

1938

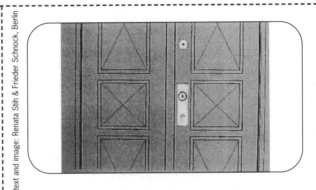

© text and image: Renata Stih & Frieder Schnock, Berlin

Kennzeichnungszwang für Wohnungen jüdischer Familien durch den „Judenstern".

It is made compulsory for Jewish residences to be marked with the Star of David.

26th March 1942

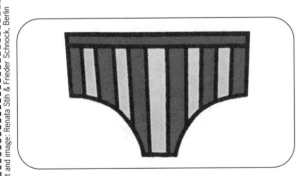

© text and image: Renata Stih & Frieder Schnock, Berlin

Berliner Badeanstalten und Schwimmbäder dürfen von Juden nicht betreten werden.

Jews are not allowed to use open-air or indoor swimming pools in Berlin.
3rd December 1938

© text and image: Renata Stih & Frieder Schnock, Berlin

Um bei den Besuchern aus dem Ausland einen schlechten Eindruck zu verhindern, sollen Schilder mit extremem Inhalt abgenommen werden; es genügen Schilder wie *Juden sind hier unerwünscht.*

In order not to give visitors from abroad a bad impression any signs with an extreme message are to be removed. It is sufficient to have signs such as 'Jews are not welcome here'. **29th January 1936**

Copy for each pupil. Cut out the four cards along the dashed lines.

© text and image: Renata Stih & Frieder Schnock, Berlin

Die in Berlin aufgestellten judenfeindlichen Schilder werden 1936 während der Olympischen Spiele vorübergehend entfernt.

The anti-Jewish posters put up in Berlin are to be temporarily removed during the Olympic Games in 1936.

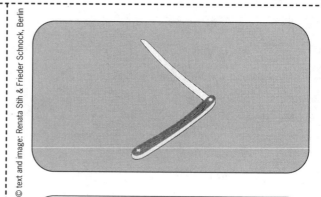

© text and image: Renata Stih & Frieder Schnock, Berlin

Juden sollen keine Seife und Rasierseife mehr erhalten.

Jews are no longer to receive soap and shaving soap.
12th June 1941

© text and image: Renata Stih & Frieder Schnock, Berlin

Juden dürfen öffentliche Verkehrsmittel nur noch auf dem Weg zur Arbeit benutzen. Vollständiges Benutzungsverbot.

Jews are only allowed to use public transport on their way to work.
13th September 1941
All use of public transport is prohibited.
24th April 1942

© text and image: Renata Stih & Frieder Schnock, Berlin

Juden dürfen nach 8 Uhr abends (im Sommer 9 Uhr) ihre Wohnungen nicht mehr verlassen.

Jews are no longer allowed to leave their homes after 8pm (or 9pm in the summer).
1st September 1939

Copy for each pupil. Cut out the four cards along the dashed lines.

© text and image: Renata Stih & Frieder Schnock, Berlin

Eheschließungen und außerehelicher Verkehr zwischen Staatsangehörigen deutschen Blutes und Juden werden mit Zuchthaus bestraft. Trotzdem geschlossene Ehen sind ungültig.

Marriages and extra-marital affairs between nationals of German stock and Jews are punishable by imprisonment. As of today, mixed marriages are not valid.
15th September 1935

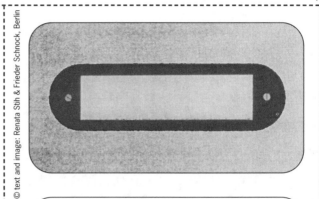

© text and image: Renata Stih & Frieder Schnock, Berlin

Juden kann ohne Angabe von Gründen und ohne Einhaltung von Fristen die Wohnung gekündigt werden.

Jews can be evicted from their homes without a reason being given and without the terms of notice being served.
30th April 1939

© text and image: Renata Stih & Frieder Schnock, Berlin

Lebensmittel dürfen Juden in Berlin nur nachmittags von 4–5 Uhr einkaufen.

Jews are only allowed to make purchases of groceries in Berlin between 4pm and 5pm.
4th July 1940

© text and image: Renata Stih & Frieder Schnock, Berlin

Juden dürfen keine Zeitungen und Zeitschriften mehr kaufen.

Jews are no longer allowed to buy newspapers and magazines.
17th February 1942

35

You will need

- pens or pencils
- large sheets of paper

♦ **HISTORY DICTIONARY**

The important words	My explanation of them
eyewitness	_____
death camps	_____

What did Hitler do to the Jews of Europe during the Second World War?

As Adolf Hitler took over more and more countries in Europe, more Jews came under his control. From 1940 onwards, Hitler used three main ways to murder them.

Stage 1 500,000 Jews were walled up in ghettos and left to die from starvation and disease.

Stage 2 Two million Jews were taken from their homes by a specially trained force called the SS Einsatzgruppe. They were lined up and shot. Their bodies were thrown into huge burial pits.

Stage 3 Nearly four million Jews were sent to concentration camps or specially built **death camps**. They were gassed, or starved or worked to death.

Stage 1: The ghettos

The largest Jewish ghetto was in Warsaw in Poland. Hitler realised that if he stopped the Jews from looking like human beings, it would help to make non-Jews think they were killing dangerous animals like rats and snakes. Hitler:

- forced all Jews into a tiny section of the city of Warsaw and then built a huge wall to stop them getting out and 'infecting' the non-Jews
- made at least seven people live in every room
- allowed them only 300 calories of food per day (this is the equivalent of two slices of bread and margarine – and nothing else)
- wouldn't allow heating in any of the houses
- allowed dirty water to enter the washing and drinking systems of the ghetto
- took all their money, belongings and jobs.

How long do you think your own families could survive in these sorts of conditions?

Your task

Work with a partner.

1. Examine Sources 1–3 on page 2 and discuss them with your partner. When you have done this, complete the task below.
2. You are a Red Cross worker. Use the information in Sources 1–3 to design a poster or slogan, or to write a speech, poem or song to let the world know what is happening in the ghettos.

SOURCE 1 A description of life in the Warsaw Ghetto by a visitor

On the streets children are crying in vain, children who are dying of hunger. They howl, beg, sing, moan, shiver with cold, without underwear, without clothing, without shoes, in rags, sacks, flannel which are bound in strips around their skeletons, children swollen with hunger, half conscious. Already completely grown up at the age of five, gloomy and weary of life. Every day and every night hundreds of these children die.

I no longer look at the people; when I hear groaning and sobbing I cross the road.

SOURCE 2 The Germans organised coach tours through the ghetto. This account was written by Albert Rosenberg, a leading Nazi who went on one of the tours

Seeing this race which is decaying, decomposing and rotten to the core will stop anyone having any sympathy for the Jews.

It is the state rubbish dump. Five to six thousand die each month.

In answer to my question whether it was reckoned that in ten years time the Jews would all have died, Dr Frank said he did not want to wait such a long time.

SOURCE 3 Line drawing from a photograph of a Jewish child begging in the streets of the Warsaw Ghetto

Stage 2: The SS Einsatzgruppe: the death squads

Your task A

Read Source 4. You will find it difficult to believe that anyone could do these things to other human beings. But this is an **eyewitness** account written by a German builder. It is almost certainly true.

SOURCE 4

The people who had got off the lorries – men, women and children of all ages had to undress on the orders of an SS man who was carrying a dog whip in his hand. Without weeping or crying these people undressed and stood together in family groups, embracing each other and saying good-bye. I did not hear a single plea for mercy. I watched a family of about eight. A woman with snow-white hair held a one-year-old child in her arms singing to it and tickling it. The child squeaked with delight. The father held a ten-year-old boy by the hand speaking softly to him. The boy was struggling to hold back his tears. The father pointed a finger to the sky and stroked his head, and seemed to be explaining something to him. The SS man counted off some twenty people. I walked up to the huge grave. The bodies were lying so tightly packed that only their heads showed, from almost all of which blood ran over their shoulders. Some were still moving. There were about 1000 bodies. An SS man sat, legs swinging on the edge of the ditch. He had an automatic rifle. He was smoking a cigarette. The people, completely naked, climbed down steps, stumbled over the heads of those lying there and stopped at the spot indicated by the SS man. They lay down. Then I heard a series of rifle shots. I looked in the ditch and saw bodies contorting.

Your task B

1. Discuss Source 4 with your partner. Between you, underline those parts of the source which you think show that the Jews NEVER lost their human spirit.

One ten-year-old boy, Elie Wiesel, saw most of his family die like this, in front of his own eyes. Then for some unknown reason:
'Two steps from the pit we were ordered to turn to the left and made to go into a barracks. We were not yet due for the "selection".'

2. Try to put yourself in Elie Wiesel's shoes. Describe his thoughts and feelings as:
- he watched his family being murdered
- he waited in the queue for his turn to be shot
- he was turned away and sent to the barracks.

'I never saw a single one of the victims weep.' Elie's story

_____

_____

_____

_____

_____

_____

_____

_____

_____

_____

_____

_____

_____

_____

_____

☞

Stage 3: The death camps

As you read or listen to this true story, try to imagine what you would have felt like if you had been in Regina's shoes. When this story is over, look at the task on page 11.

Story: A survivor from the death camps

Regina Franks was born in Poland in 1926. Her parents were Jewish. In December 1939, Regina's father was rounded up by the SS Einsatzgruppe, forced to dig his own grave and then shot in the back of the head. In June 1942 Regina's mother, brother and two sisters were transported to Belzec from where no one came back. Regina was imprisoned in Frankfurt from July 1942 to February 1943. From there she was taken to Auschwitz. She stayed there for nearly two years. In January 1945, Regina was part of a convoy of prisoners leaving Auschwitz on what has become known as the 'death march'. She travelled partly on foot to Gross Rosen, then by open wagon to Mauthausen, and finally to Bergen-Belsen by train. The camp was eventually liberated on 15 April 1945.

Regina spoke German, Polish and Russian. This made her useful to the Nazis as an interpreter and a Lauferin *(messenger girl). By sheer luck, together with an iron determination, Regina survived.*

Here is a selection of her memories.

On entering Auschwitz

Our convoy of 160 prisoners arrived in the middle of the night. As we got down from the trucks, we had no real idea of what was to happen next. We began filing in through the gates. Just ahead of us, inside the gates, were three men. They were hanging from some wooden gallows.

I knew I was in hell.

A few days later, Doctor Mengele was ready to sort the Jews who were chosen to live from those who would go straight to the gas chambers. Mengele stood there with a riding crop in his hand. He ordered us to line up and to slowly walk in front of him. He looked us up and down and then pointed with his crop. Some went to the right, some went to the left. The line of people sent to

the right was much longer than the line sent to the left. All the children went to the right. All the old people too.

To the right, to the left, to the right, to the left, to death to life. To the gas chambers, to the reception barracks. I was sent to the left . . . inside the huge gates, past the three men hanging, and over to the barracks. Out of 160 people on the convoy, only 20 were sent to the left. I thanked God for the person who had told me: 'Scrape your nails on the inside of your hand until it draws blood. Then wipe the blood on your cheeks. It will make you look healthy. The Nazis want healthy, strong people to work for them.'

I remember a time when Mengele was going through the selection process with

☞ another convoy of Jews. As the people chosen to go into the showers were filing into the shower rooms, one woman had hidden her baby inside the sleeve of her jacket. It started crying. She raised her baby up and begged a German guard to save it. He lifted his bayonet and drove it through the baby's heart.

Their intention was to dehumanise us. They took our clothes and made us stand naked. Each person stepped forward to have a number tattooed on their wrist. Mine was 34679. Then they shaved all our hair off. We huddled together to keep warm and to protect our modesty. A German guard began laughing at us.

'You will soon forget that behaviour.' he laughed. 'Soon you will behave like animals to each other. Then you will die.'

I looked at him and said, 'There is a saying, "Clothes make people", but I personally have never believed that.'

He looked hard at me. 'Fighting words for a Jew,' he said. 'But I won't kill you yet. I shall wait two weeks. Then I will come and find you . . . if you are still alive.' I knew then that I would live. Never, never would this man have the satisfaction of seeing my corpse.

A guard handed out our camp clothes: a coarse cotton jacket; a pair of trousers; no underwear. Nothing to protect our skin from the lice which, as our bodies warmed up, jumped from the seams of the clothes and burrowed beneath our skin. A large bundle of wooden clogs was thrown into the middle of the floor. Everyone scrambled to find a pair that fitted. Not

that it really mattered. All that these so-called shoes were was a wooden sole with two straps of cloth sewn across for you to slide your feet into.

After the shaving, and then the issue of camp clothes, we were allocated our huts. I was in a hut with other Poles. I soon found out what the German officer meant when he said that we would become like animals. This was their intention. We were each made to share a bunk with eight other people. These had originally been stalls for horses; one horse to each stall. We were given a bowl to collect our soup and bread rations, and a spoon to eat with. Woe betide you if you lost these essentials. Nobody could help you. No bowl, no soup. It was as simple as that. Since soup and bread were the only things we ever ate, the loss of a soup bowl was catastrophic. When a person died during the night, there was a scramble to take their bowl and spoon. The bowl might be marginally bigger than yours. There might even be some scraps of food left in the bottom. But the living didn't fight one another for bread or soup. The Nazis weren't able to dehumanise us that much.

Staying alive

I was determined to survive at Auschwitz. I was determined to prove the SS guard wrong. One night, I had been lucky enough to steal a square of black bread from the stores where I happened to be working as a cleaner and interpreter for all the Russian prisoners. In Auschwitz, anything we got like that wasn't called stealing, it was called 'organising'. I hid it

☞ inside my jacket to eat in the morning when I knew I would be really hungry. Then I folded the jacket up, as usual, to use as my pillow. When I woke up the next morning, the bread had disappeared. There were a series of holes in my jacket. I realised what had happened. During the night, a rat had gnawed through my 'pillow' and eaten all the bread.

After that, if I managed to 'organise' any food, I ate it as soon as I could. I also learned to share my spoils with the other people in my block. One time it was margarine that I 'organised'. I was working in the kitchens at the time. I hid it under my jacket and then realised that it was melting. You can imagine my horror when I saw that the guards were searching everyone as they left the building. I really thought that I was 'for it' that time. Miraculously, they got bored with this task about ten people in front of me. The margarine was running slowly down the inside of my leg but somehow I got past them and back to the block with my precious cargo.

Another time I was able to 'organise' a heel of bread to be taken to a man who had been put in solitary confinement for some supposed misdemeanour. Years later we met up again. He bought me a gold watch, just to say thank you for my kindness.

Sometimes my overwhelming desire to survive led me to do things which, in later years, I felt really guilty about. Now, however, I know I have no need to feel guilty. I only did what anyone else in my position would have done and it means I am still alive to tell the truth about the Nazi death camps.

One day, I was working in the 'Officers Mess', cleaning up their dining area. I overheard them discussing which barracks would be cleared in the morning. Mine was one of them. I knew what this meant. We would get an early morning call, supposedly to go and be deloused and disinfected at the camp baths. There we would be told to get undressed, fold our clothes up neatly and walk into the so-called shower rooms. The door would slam shut behind us. We would look up and see the shower heads. Most of us would know exactly what was going to happen. Some wouldn't. Some would have refused to believe that anyone could be so inhuman.

Then the smell would waft over. Slowly, steadily, the hiss of gas escaping. Then the choking sensation. People clinging to each other, gasping for breath, reaching up for air. After fifteen minutes all of them would be dead. Then, later, those of us who had escaped death for a while longer, would see the flames rising high into the sky and the stench of burning flesh would steal into our senses.

What should I do? If I told them all, everyone would try to disappear when the call came. If I kept quiet, then maybe I could slip out at night and sleep somewhere else. It was my birthday. I was seventeen years old and I didn't want to die.

That night I waited till everyone was asleep. Then I crept outside. I slipped over to the nearest barracks. It was full of

Poles: non-Jewish Poles. They drove me out. So I crept over to another barracks. This time it was full of Czechoslovakians. I crawled underneath one of the bunk beds and lay down on the filthy muddy ground. All night the rats scurried all over me. But I was alive. I had beaten the Germans once again. The people from my barracks got their call up that morning.

The triumph of good over evil

Being at Auschwitz was like being in hell. I knew that as soon as I arrived and I had seen the three men hanging from the gallows. I remember so many dreadful things. But I remember equally as clearly so many kind, good and unselfish acts from people I hardly knew, who were surviving in just as appalling conditions as myself. I am alive today because of these simple acts of human kindness and because the Nazis failed to destroy the essence of humanity, our human spirit.

Every morning we were woken up to attend roll call. There were several thousand prisoners in the camp at any one time. We all had to go outside and line up one behind the other. We had to stand like this until every single inmate of the camp had been counted. This included all those who had died during the night. They too had to be carried out and counted. Sometimes this would take up to five hours. You can imagine how we felt in the middle of winter. The people in my hut used to help one another. We would stand as close to the person in front as we could

and then we would use our warm breath to breathe onto the back of their necks. Everyone would take it in turn to stand at the very back of the line, where there was no one to warm your neck for you. So you see, we were beating the Nazis yet again. We kept our humanity.

I remember the time when I caught malaria. The disease made me shake and shiver so much that at one point I actually wanted to die. But the Russian prisoners with whom I worked and acted as an interpreter were determined that I should stay alive. Every morning when roll call came around they came and hoisted me out of bed. One of them would tie my ankles onto her ankles. Another one would tie my wrists onto her wrists. That way they could hide my shaking from the Nazis.

After a while it became obvious that I wasn't getting any better. One of them had a Czechoslovakian friend who worked in the stores. We called this place 'Canada', because, in eastern European countries, Canada had always been seen as the land of plenty. She persuaded her to steal ('organise') some quinine and a syringe. I can't remember her name, but her kindness saved my life. Every night until the quinine ran out, I injected myself. There were no antiseptic facilities so I used to urinate on the needle to disinfect it. It worked and I am still here today, thanks to the humanity of my fellow prisoners.

As a *Lauferin* or messenger girl, I would stand at the gates to receive messages from the work stations where the SS

guards stayed. I would take the messages from one camp station to another. One day, early in 1945, when the camp was alive with rumours that the Russians were advancing towards us, I recognised two former friends from my old school. They were with their mother, Mrs Lerner. But my two friends had been told that they were being sent to an ammunition centre in another camp. 'Please look after our mother,' they whispered as they went through the gates.

The next evening I went to find the mother. She was lying on her bed. I noticed that she had a huge gangrenous ulcer on her shin. She had fallen and scraped her leg. The sore had never healed. Over the next few days, the woman grew more and more ill. She became delirious. There seemed to be nothing I could do. But I knew of a Russian prisoner who worked as a doctor in the camp, so I went to see her. 'My aunt' (I lied) 'is in terrible pain. You must come and see her.'

I took the doctor across to where the woman was lying. 'There is no hope,' the doctor said. 'She has gangrene. We need to amputate her leg.'

'Then do it,' I cried.

'But my dear,' she said, 'I have no anaesthetics. I have no surgical instruments. She will die.'

'Do you remember swearing the Hippocratic Oath?' I replied. 'It is your duty to try to save a life. If you do it, then at least we will have tried.'

Somehow the Russian doctor managed to 'organise' what was necessary and the operation took place. The next evening I visited the woman. She was still alive . . . and the next . . . and the next. Then it was my turn to leave the camp. So I took as much bread and water across to Mrs Lerner as I could 'organise'. I said goodbye, and left her, as I thought to die. Amazingly, this woman survived her amputation, for the camp was liberated by the Russians a few days later and she was able to receive proper hospital treatment.

Leaving Auschwitz

During the final months of 1944, the SS were preoccupied with destroying all evidence of Hitler's 'Final Solution'. The gas chambers were destroyed, the ground was levelled and trees were planted in their place. Then they began emptying the camp of all remaining prisoners. Each day, fresh convoys of prisoners were sent off in cattle trucks to an unknown destination. When, in January 1945, it was my turn to be moved, the SS had run out of trucks so our convoy was forced to set off on foot. We had no idea where we were going, or how long it would take.

For the entire march, we had only our wooden clogs and our camp uniforms. No coats, no warmer clothing, no boots. Every time the Russian planes flew overhead, we had to hide in ditches by the side of the road. Many people, once they had laid down, were too ill to stand up again. So the SS guards shot them.

It was on this march that I encountered human kindness from the strangest source

35

☞

of all. One evening, the line of 'refugees' was approaching a small village. We were mortally cold and hungry. A female guard, SS Baker, called me out of line to ask about some of the other female prisoners from the kitchens. I couldn't answer her, but by the time she had finished with me, the line had moved on. So she took me to a small cottage at the edge of the village where some of the guards were to spend the night. Her husband was also a guard. He opened the door.

'You have a dirty Jew with you,' her husband hissed. 'Why don't we shoot her?'

'She is in my charge,' SS Baker replied, 'and I will make sure that she remains unharmed.'

That night I slept in a bed alongside three female German SS guards. Yet again my life was saved by an act of kindness. And this person was German, the enemy of all Jews.

Because we had lost sight of the other prisoners, I was taken to a nearby town. The rest of the journey to a place called Gross Rosen was by train. I remember to this day where I slept at night. I was curled up inside the mesh luggage holders which extended from the wall. It was like sleeping in a hammock and so much more comfortable than the tiered bunks we had at Auschwitz. Apparently, Hitler needed to transport so many wounded troops from the front line that he commandeered all the cattle trucks. Experience had taught him, you see, that these cattle trucks could carry many more human beings than an ordinary train!

The journey from Gross Rosen to Mauthausen

The guard SS Baker and myself joined the convoy of prisoners at Gross Rosen. By this time, our numbers had decreased dramatically. Almost immediately, we were on the move again; this time by cattle truck to a men's camp called Mauthausen. The guards knew where we were going, of course, but we prisoners had no idea of our destination or how long it would take us to get there.

The cattle trucks which transported us to Mauthausen were the most basic imaginable. Inside each wagon, which was open to the sky, there was no sanitation, apart from a bucket which was soon filled with excrement. It slid wildly from one end of the wagon, to the other. There was no food, and no shelter from the hail and snow which hit us as we passed through Austria. Many people died in the cattle trucks. We were not even allowed to throw them out of the trucks. They would have been evidence of Hitler's inhumanity, which the Nazis were desperate to hide from the approaching British and Russian troops.

Bergen-Belsen

In February 1945, after a two-week stay in Mauthausen, those of us who were still alive finally arrived by ordinary train at Bergen-Belsen. I was there for two months. The War was coming to an end and the Germans knew they had lost. So the inmates of the camp were just left to die. After five months, people were dying at the rate of 500 a day, mostly from typhus or

typhoid. I thanked God for my mother who, when we were small, had insisted on all four children being vaccinated against typhus and typhoid. I was the only one left to benefit from her foresight . . .

Liberation

On 15 April 1945, the British liberated Belsen. I remember the moment the first soldiers walked through the gates of the camp. A prisoner was kneeling just outside these gates. He had a human ear in his mouth, but he was too exhausted even to chew it. The final few days before liberation had seen many prisoners desperately trying to stay alive by eating the flesh of their dead comrades. I couldn't condemn them. I had managed to eat by raiding the stores which, thanks to the fact that the guards were deserting their posts in droves, had been unattended. Even then, all that had been available to me were some extremely hard and dry swedes.

The next thing I remember is climbing up one of the watch towers with as big a block of concrete as I could manage to carry. I wanted to drop it onto the head of the camp doctor, Doctor König. But something stopped me. I could not do it. Even after everything I had gone through I knew it was wrong to deliberately harm another human being. I knew that if I did, then the Nazis would have won. They would have dehumanised me after all.

After the liberation

For many months I lay ill with malaria, hepatitis and dysentery inside the field-

hospital that the British had erected. When I recovered, I met one of the soldiers working there. Some time later we were married.

People often ask me if I can forgive the Nazis for what happened. This is what I say to them. I can try to forgive what they did to me, but I have no right to forgive, nor to forget, what they did to my mother, father, two sisters and brother. Only they can forgive. My mother and father had always taught me that the person who hates is eventually destroyed by his own hatred. I lost all hope in Auschwitz and Bergen-Belsen, but I never lost my human spirit. I never lost my sense of what is right and wrong and I never learned to hate as Hitler and the Nazis hated.

Your task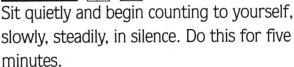

Sit quietly and begin counting to yourself, slowly, steadily, in silence. Do this for five minutes.

If you counted like this, all day and every day, it would take you six full months to count up to four million, which is the number of Jews who were murdered in the death camps.

Despite such suffering, Regina Franks says that the prisoners never lost their humanity. Read the story again and underline all the moments when the prisoners showed their true humanity. Then choose one of the moments to illustrate as a message of hope to the world.

36

You will need

- pen or pencil

How did the Oppenheimers suffer during the Holocaust?

The Oppenheimer family had a different experience from that of Regina Franks. Regina was the only one of her family to survive. Until the day she died, Regina felt lost, lonely and in despair.

All three Oppenheimer children survived. Paul's story below tells you what happened to them and the rest of their family. Read the story and then complete the task on pages 3–5.

Story: The journey to Westerbork, June 1943

Very early one Sunday morning in June 1943, my father heard a loud knock on the door. When he went to open the door, two German soldiers (they were called the SS) stood there.

'You have thirty minutes in which to pack your belongings and gather in the square over there. All the Jews in this area are being sent to a camp in Westerbork. Hurry up or there'll be trouble.'

Mother and Father looked dreadful. It was obvious that they were very worried. So was I. But at least I knew my grandparents would be coming with us and that everyone else would be Jewish too. At least we would be amongst friends.

We took our best and our warmest clothes. My poor little sister Eve wore about four pairs of socks and goodness knows how many vests. Rudi and I had our newest shirts and trousers and the warmest hats and coats we could find. It was so hot! After all, it was the middle of June. But as Mother said, we would be staying at Westerbork till the end of the War and nobody knew how long that would be.

When we arrived at Westerbork, I must admit I was very frightened. It looked just like a prison. There were guards everywhere and the camp was surrounded by huge barbed wire fences. I was glad of all the extra clothes that Mother had made us wear, because at night it got very cold.

The worst thing about Westerbork was waiting for Monday evenings. Every Monday, a list of about 1000 names would be pinned on the wall. If your name was on that list, it meant you were being sent to another camp. These camps were too dreadful to even think about, for when you arrived at one of these camps, the German soldiers were waiting to kill you.

About a week after we had arrived, the list was published. I read through it as quickly as possible. Thank God. Mother, Father, Rudi and Eve and myself were not on the list. But then my blood froze. There were the names of our beloved grandparents. Father and Mother just looked at each other. Eve burst into tears, whilst Rudi and I like typical boys just looked at the ground.

I never saw my grandparents again. I know they died as soon as they reached the next camp, because it was a place called Sobibor and out of 34,000 people who went there, only 19 came back alive.

I know, too, that they would have been very brave. No one would ever let the soldiers see how afraid they were. Grandpa would have held Grandma very tightly. Granddad Oppenheimer (my father's father) would have laughed and teased Granny right to the end and I know too that they would have been thinking about us and praying that God would not allow the soldiers to do the same thing to the rest of their family.

For the next few months Mother, Father and we three children managed well enough. Sometimes I could almost begin to believe we were going to be all right. But something kept niggling in the back of my mind. I remembered that picture of Adolf Hitler which had hung on the wall of my classroom in Germany. His eyes seemed to follow you everywhere. Somehow I knew that his eyes were following me and my family. Somehow I knew that our journey hadn't ended at all. In fact, the worst part of the journey was just about to begin.

The journey to Bergen-Belsen, February 1944

On the morning of 1 February 1944, our names appeared on the 'list'. Taking what was left of our belongings, the whole family was put on a train and sent to a concentration camp called Bergen-Belsen. Before we got there none of us knew what to expect. There were rumours, of course, about factory chimneys belching out foul-smelling smoke day and night. Some people said that every single child who went to one of these camps was sent to the bath house to be scrubbed and cleaned and was never heard of again. These rumours were so silly and preposterous that no one really believed them. Or did they?

We soon found out what Bergen-Belsen was like. There were no factory chimneys there, no bath houses. The Nazis didn't need them. Conditions in the camp were so bad that the soldiers didn't even try to kill people. They were just left to die from starvation or disease.

Every single morning we were woken early to get up for 'appell' or roll call. The soldiers made us stand outside in the freezing cold for up to five hours whilst they checked up on all the people who were ill or had died in the night. Then we had breakfast. This was a mug of brown liquid called 'ersatz kaffee' or pretend coffee! There was no bread or cereal, just a drink.

The adults then had to go and work in the fields. The children didn't have to work. We actually did nothing all day because we were too tired from lack of food to think of anything to occupy the time. At lunchtime we all queued for a bowl of turnip soup. Again there was no bread, just soup. In the evening, each person was allowed a four-centimetre-square piece of black bread. That was our daily ration in the camp.

After the 'evening meal' the family was allowed to meet up. This was a very important time for us all. Mother and Eve could tell us what had happened and who had been taken ill. Father, Rudi and myself could do the same. Then we would plan what we would do as a family once the War was over.

One day in January 1945, almost a year after we had arrived at Bergen-Belsen, my mother was taken ill. She was moved into the hospital barracks. We used to visit her every night. But there weren't any medicines and of course she wasn't given any extra food to help her. Soon after entering hospital, Mother died. I don't remember feeling particularly sad. I suppose it was because everyone's parents were dying. It must have been worse for my little sister Eve, because there was nobody to look after her in the women's camp any more.

A few weeks later, my father went into the same hospital. He died. I was too tired and ill myself to even realise that I was now the oldest member of the Oppenheimer family. Father, Mother, Granny, Granddad, Grandma and Grandpa; Hitler had got them all. I was sixteen years old and the only person left who could look after Rudi and Eve.

By now there was an epidemic of typhoid fever. Every day about 500 people were dying. Those people who were still alive were too weak and ill to bury the dead bodies. So they removed what little clothing the bodies had on them, and piled up all the bodies against the walls of the sleeping huts. The children were given a new job. We had to hunt for the lice that lived in the clothes of the dead people and then squash them because it was the lice that caused the fever.

Your task

'Rudi and I like typical boys just looked at the ground.'
This is how Paul Oppenheimer described the moment he read that his grandparents were being sent to the gas chambers.

1. Why would Paul and Rudi try to hide their feelings from their parents and little sister Eve?

Paul and Rudi probably tried to hide their feelings so that _____

_____

_____

_____

_____

_____

_____

〰〰〰〰〰〰〰〰〰〰〰〰〰〰〰〰〰〰〰〰〰〰〰〰〰〰〰〰〰〰〰〰

_____

_____

_____

_____

2. What do you think Paul and Rudi were really thinking?

I think Paul and Rudi were _____

_____

_____

_____

_____

_____

_____

_____

_____

_____

_____

3. Towards the end of the story Paul's mother Rita died. His little sister Eve was left alone in the women's camp. Imagine you are Eve. She still talked to her mother as if she were alive. What would Eve have talked about?
(Use the template on page 5 to help you to imagine how Eve was feeling.)

To my dearest Mother

All my love
Eve

37

You will need

- pen or pencil

Why did so many Jews starve in the death camps?

Adolf Hitler wanted to starve the Jews to death. He also wanted them to work: digging, building, making roads, and doing similar jobs. So Hitler asked his doctors to work out a diet which would keep people just strong enough to work for three or four weeks but slowly starve them to death.

When the Jews arrived at the concentration camps, the guards gave each person just enough food to keep them alive for a short time. Once they had died of starvation, another truckload of Jews arrived and the same thing happened all over again.

Your task

You could work with a partner for this task.

In Paul's story, he tells you how much food he was allowed.

1. Find the section of Paul's story which describes his diet.
2. Complete this 'diet sheet' for Bergen-Belsen Star Camp children. (You could ask someone from the Food Technology department to help you to work out how many calories Paul and his family were allowed.)

Bergen-Belsen Concentration Camp: Daily rations for Jews		
Meal	Menu	Number of calories

3. Below is a chart showing the typical daily rations for British civilians during the War. Find out the number of calories they received each day.

Daily rations for the average civilian in wartime Britain		
Meal	Menu	Number of calories
Breakfast	porridge fresh or stewed fruit bread and butter with marmalade milk to drink or tea	120 75 150 milk = 250 tea = 20
Dinner	sausages raisin dumplings with golden syrup	180 340
Tea/Supper	blackberry bake wholemeal bread and butter cocoa	260 100 230
	Total number of calories =	

☞ 4. Using the chart below, draw up a list of what a typical teenager nowadays will eat during the day using the table below. Be honest. Don't forget all the snacks and drinks that you have between meals!

Typical daily diet of an average British teenager in the 1990s		
Meal	Menu	Number of calories
Breakfast		
Snack		
Dinner		
Snack		
Tea		
Snack		

💬 ■ How would you have felt if you only had as much food as Paul, Rudi and Eve?
■ One of Rudi's jobs was to dole out the bowls of soup. Often all the vegetables would sink to the bottom of the pan. What would you do if you were Rudi, giving soup to all the children in the camp?
■ How do you think ordinary British teenagers would have felt about their diet during wartime? (Remember, some of them had grown up knowing nothing else.)

CONCLUSION
How did the Second World War end?

On 6 June 1944 soldiers from the different countries that were fighting against Germany landed in France. Over the next few months they moved closer and closer to Germany. Russian soldiers were also moving closer to Germany from the other side of Europe. The map below shows you what was happening.

By April 1945 the War with Germany was over. The Allies had won. On 30 April Adolf Hitler committed suicide.

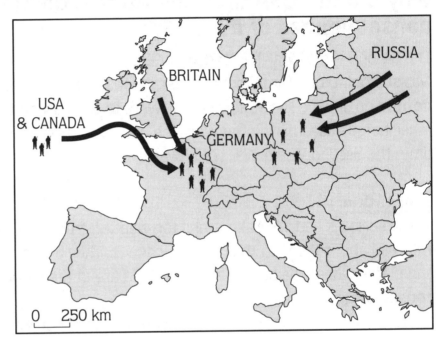

Allied troops moving towards Germany, June 1944

But there was still a war going on with Japan. The map below shows you where the country of Japan is. It is separated from America by the Pacific Ocean.

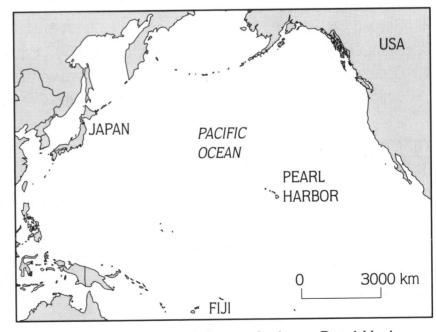

Most of the fighting against Japan took place around the Pacific Ocean

In 1941 the Japanese had attacked the American naval fleet at its base, Pearl Harbor. The two countries had been at war ever since. Great Britain was on the side of the Americans. Germany had supported the Japanese.

38

You will need
- pen or pencil

◆ **HISTORY DICTIONARY**

The important words	My explanation of them
atomic bomb	_____
	_____

Why did the USA drop the atomic bomb and what were the consequences of it?

The Second World War had ended in Europe on 8 May 1945. The war against Japan was still going on. Three months later, it was over. The USA dropped two huge **atomic bombs** on Japan. The atomic bombs were two thousand times the strength of any other bombs used during the War. The Japanese surrendered on 14 August 1945. This time, the Second World War really was over.

Your task A

The Americans had several reasons for wanting to drop these bombs on Japan. You will read about them on the chart on page 2. They are in the **causes** column. The dates and places where the bombs were dropped are in the **events** column. The **consequences** column is empty.

1. Read Sources 1–6 on page 3. As you read each source, underline each consequence or result of dropping the bomb that you can find.
2. Record each consequence in the correct column of the chart.
3. Compare your list of consequences with a friend's list.
4. Decide between you which were the short-term consequences of the bomb and which were the long-term consequences. Write ST or LT in the final column.

Your task B

Decide which was the most dreadful consequence of the bomb. Write a short newspaper report explaining what it was and how you feel about it.

The Americans stopped letting journalists visit Hiroshima. Why do you think they did this?

〰〰

After you have read Sources 1–6 on page 3, record all the consequences in the column on the chart below. When you have decided whether it was a short- or long-term consequence, write ST or LT in the final column.

Causes	Events	Consequences	Short-term or long-term?
The Americans thought that the Japanese would never surrender.	On 6 August 1945, an American bomber dropped the world's first atomic bomb on the Japanese city of Hiroshima.		
If the US army invaded Japan, hundreds of thousands of American soldiers might be killed.	On 9 August 1945 another American bomber dropped the world's second atomic bomb on the Japanese city of Nagasaki.		
The atomic bomb had cost 2 thousand million dollars to develop. The Americans didn't want to waste all this money.			
The atomic bomb was a way of showing the Communists in the USSR that the USA was stronger than them.			
The Japanese had been very cruel to American prisoners of war. Some people wanted to pay them back.			

SOURCE 1 From a school textbook, 1993

A Japanese journalist described a glaring pinkish light in the sky which burned people's eyes out. Anyone within a kilometre of the explosion became a bundle of smoking black charcoal within seconds. Within minutes about 70,000 people were dead. Those who were still alive writhed in agony from their burns. Then there was the blast wave, which destroyed 70,000 of the city's 78,000 buildings.

SOURCE 2 From a school textbook, 1993

Three days later, the USA dropped another bomb on Nagasaki. About 36,000 people were killed.
On 14 August 1945 Japan surrendered.

SOURCE 3 From J. Hersey's account of the effects of the bomb, published in 1946

Father Kleinsorge found about twenty men in the bushes. They were all in the same nightmarish state: their faces were wholly burned, their eye sockets hollow, the fluid from their melted eyes had run down their cheeks. Their mouths were swollen, pus-covered wounds, which they could not stretch enough to get round the spout of a teapot.

SOURCE 4 An eyewitness account from a five-year-old girl

The skin was burned off some of them and was hanging from their hands and from their chins.

SOURCE 5 Three weeks later, a British journalist managed to get to Hiroshima. He wrote the first public account of radiation sickness. It appeared in the *Daily Express*

In Hiroshima, 30 days later, people who were not injured in the bombing are still dying mysteriously and horribly from an unknown something which I can only describe as the atomic plague.

SOURCE 6 A Japanese eyewitness account of radiation sickness

Survivors began to notice in themselves a strange form of illness. It consisted of vomiting, loss of appetite, diarrhoea with large amounts of blood, purple spots on the skin, bleeding from the mouth, loss of hair and usually death.

Should the Americans have dropped the atomic bomb?

Your task

Look carefully at the cartoon above and then discuss the questions below as a whole class.

1. **What is the cartoon saying?**
2. **Can you trust this cartoon?**
3. **If the reasons in the cartoon for dropping the bomb were the real ones, do you think the Americans were right to drop it on Japan?**
   Read your causes and consequences page again.
4. **Do you think the American scientists knew what would happen when they dropped the bomb?**
5. **Are any of the reasons that the Americans gave for dropping the bomb justified?**

39

You will need

- pen or pencil

◆ **HISTORY DICTIONARY**

The important words	My explanation of them
nuclear missile	_____
	_____
invention	_____
	_____
discovery	_____
	_____

Technology, transport and two world wars

During the twentieth century, there have been dramatic changes in technology and transport. New weapons such as **nuclear missiles** have been developed. Many of the changes happened because countries needed new ways to win wars.

How good are you at working out how and why each new **invention** or **discovery** helped to win wars?

Your task

Work in pairs. Use the invention cards on page 3.

1. Record each invention on the timeline provided on page 2.
2. Use reference books from the library to find out **who** invented them and **what** they were used for.
3. Add this information to your timeline.
4. Discuss each invention with your partner.
5. In the space provided, explain how and why you think each invention was useful in trying to win a war.

☞

Technology and transport timeline

Date and name of invention or discovery	Details of invention or discovery	How and why it would help in wartime

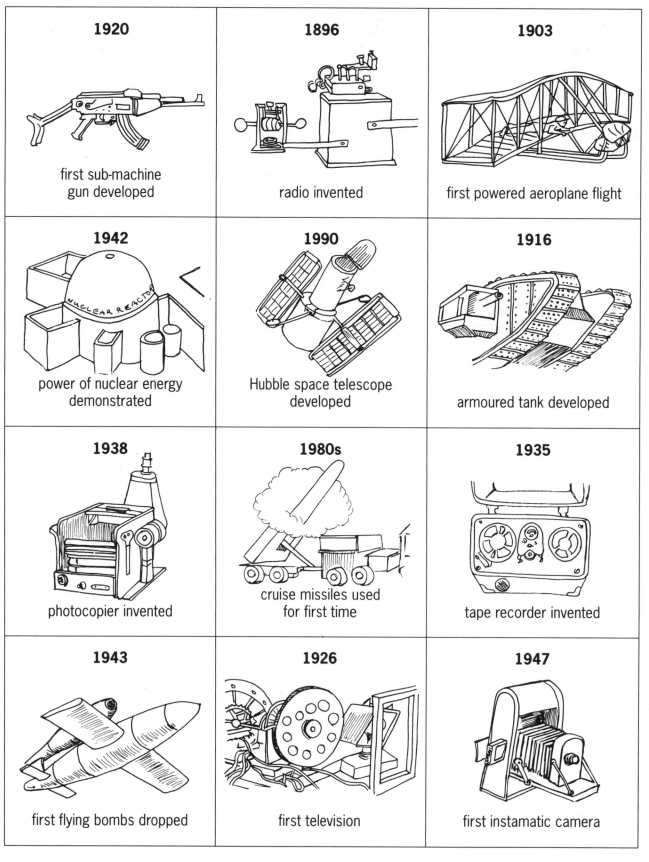

1920	**1896**	**1903**
first sub-machine gun developed	radio invented	first powered aeroplane flight
1942	**1990**	**1916**
power of nuclear energy demonstrated	Hubble space telescope developed	armoured tank developed
1938	**1980s**	**1935**
photocopier invented	cruise missiles used for first time	tape recorder invented
1943	**1926**	**1947**
first flying bombs dropped	first television	first instamatic camera

40

You will need
• pen or pencil

Looking back on the twentieth-century world

The twentieth century has seen some terrible suffering and some great cruelty. It has also seen some amazing achievements and some heroic actions. What will you choose as your important events of the century?

Your task
Work with a partner.
Use the grids below and on pages 2 and 3 to record your ideas.

What we have found out about the twentieth century

Names _____ and _____ Date _____

Main events, including wars

_____

_____

_____

_____

_____

_____

Famous people

_____

_____

_____

_____

_____

Better technology

_____

_____

_____

_____

_____

_____

  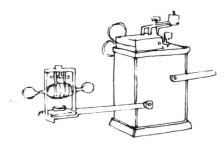

Better communications

_____

_____

_____

_____

_____

_____

☞

Terrible suffering

_____

_____

_____

_____

_____

_____

Great cruelty

_____

_____

_____

_____

_____

Your task
Record below what lessons you would like the world to learn from the events of the twentieth century.

In our opinion, the lessons we should learn from what we know about the twentieth century are _____

_____

_____

_____

_____

_____

Our children need to make sure that

_____

_____

_____

_____

_____

_____

_____

_____

_____

41

There are four pages to this task

~~~~~~

You will need

• pen or pencil

How have our towns and cities changed?

You have found out many things about the century that you were born in. Some are good. Some are bad. The events and discoveries you have learned about have changed the way people think, the way people look and the way people act. They have also changed the way places look.

Your task

Here is a list of **developments** (things which have happened) that have helped to **change** what our towns and cities look like.

Next to them is a list of **what has changed as a result** of the developments. The two lists are in the wrong order.

Draw a line from each **development** to the correct **result** of this development.

Developments

Many cities were bombed in the War and thousands of old houses were destroyed.

Cars were built very cheaply so that most people could afford to buy one.

New machines and computer technology meant that clothing and other 'consumer goods' could be made very quickly.

Faster transport, improved refrigeration and good trade links with other countries meant that traders could buy goods very cheaply and make a profit by selling huge amounts.

New medicines were discovered. People became much healthier.

More and more jobs needed doing in the cities. The government invited British families from Asia and the Caribbean to come and live in Britain to do these jobs.

Results

Small food shops disappeared. They were replaced by big 'supermarket chains'.

New houses had to be built quickly. They were called pre-fabs, because they had been pre-fabricated (already made up!).

New hospitals were built so that people could be treated for all the diseases that now had cures.

Families from all over the world, whose relatives had also fought in the War, came to live in British cities. Asian and Caribbean shops and restaurants were built, selling exotic food and clothes.

New shops and department stores opened up in the city centres, so that customers could choose from a huge range of different clothes and goods.

New roads and motorways were built to cope with a huge increase in cars, lorries and other vehicles.

Your task

Look carefully at the outline drawing below. It shows you what an ordinary town looked like in 1900. You know that towns have changed a great deal since then.

1. The drawing on page 3 shows what the same town might look like today. We have left some spaces for you to fill in, using your own knowledge. Show what has changed since 1900. Don't forget there will be more houses, new roads, different shops, more Black and Asian people as well as white people, different schools, different types of buildings, and so on.

2. For each change you have shown, write a label at the edge of the drawing to explain the change.

41

In the spaces on the outline below, draw details to show what the same town might look like today. Add a label to describe each change you have shown.

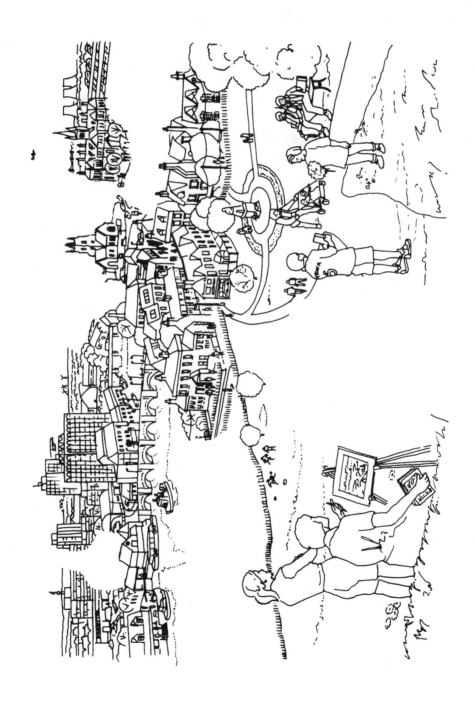

☞

Your task ✏️

When you have completed your drawing of the present-day town on page 3, imagine you are preparing a guide for visitors to this area of the town, explaining how it has changed over 100 years. Write your own explanation of:

■ three features which have changed since 1900
■ how these three features have changed since 1900.

The labels you have written around the picture on page 3 will help you to get started.

Then try to add a sentence to each change explaining why this change has happened. Your chart of developments and results (page 215) will also help.

How our towns have changed

_____

_____

_____

_____

_____

_____

_____

_____

_____

_____

_____

_____

_____

APPENDIX
Cross-unit work for all of Key Stage 3

Change and continuity: what has changed and what has stayed the same over the past 1000 years?

The following tasks have been devised so that teachers are able to develop with their pupils an understanding of the historical concept of change across the 1000-year period covered by KS3. The ideas are in no particular order and can be used in whatever way best suits the pupils. The majority of tasks require pupils to use different parts of the series picture packs. You will find full details at the beginning of the book.

You will need

- pictures of Britain 1066 to the present
- pen or pencil
- scissors
- glue

42

A thousand years of change

Your task

You could work in pairs for this activity. You are going to look at how different aspects of life have changed over one thousand years.

You could start with pictures from the four picture packs.

You could also use pictures from history textbooks, encyclopaedias, CD Roms, or other resources.

1. Choose ONE of the following aspects of life:
   - houses and homes
   - transport
   - clothing
   - violence and warfare.

2. Find pictures which show your chosen aspect.

3. Study each picture carefully, and think about what has changed about it in a thousand years.

4. Some things may not have changed at all. Think about what has stayed the same about that aspect of life.

5. Now prepare a display describing what has changed over the past thousand years. Write your own explanations of what has changed. Use your chosen pictures or outline drawings of them to help illustrate your display.

6. You should include a final paragraph explaining why you think things have changed.

43

You will need

- picture pack of your choice
- pen or pencil

Gathering evidence

When historians want to write about things that have happened in the past, some of them try to organise their evidence into four different categories.

■ **Political** evidence tells us about how a person or group of people had power over other people, groups or countries. A propaganda portrait of Adolf Hitler would be political evidence because it shows how Hitler controlled what German people thought of him.

■ **Economic** evidence tells us about money, work and how people made a living. A picture of a town market could be economic evidence.

■ **Social** evidence tells us about how ordinary people lived. A picture of the town market could therefore be social evidence as well as economic evidence!

■ **Cultural** evidence tells us about what people believed in, how they entertained themselves, and how they organised their leisure time. A picture of a wedding feast with musicians could be cultural evidence.

Your task

You should work in pairs or groups for this activity. You have only fifteen minutes to do this activity.

Which pair will be able to collect the most historical evidence in each category?

1. Choose one of the picture packs.
2. Take each picture in turn. Examine it carefully. Decide which of the four categories it gives evidence for. Remember it might give evidence for all FOUR of them.
3. Record the name and number of the picture on your chart on page 2, together with a brief explanation of why it gives evidence for a certain category. One example (from *The Twentieth-Century World*) has been done for you.
4. Make sure you do the same with each picture.

	CULTURAL	
	Name and no. of picture source	Why it gives evidence about cultural history

	SOCIAL	
	Name and no. of picture source	Why it gives evidence about social history

	ECONOMIC	
	Name and no. of picture source	Why it gives evidence about economic history

	POLITICAL	
	Name and no. of picture source	Why it gives evidence about political history
	Hitler portrait 20th C 7a	shows Hitler controlling the way young people think and act

44

There are two pages to this task

You will need
- four picture packs
- pen or pencil

When would you like to have lived?

Your task

You should work on your own for this task.

1. Look through all the picture packs and decide which of these periods you would most like to have lived in:
   ■ Medieval Realms 1066–1500
   ■ The Making of the UK 1500–1750
   ■ Britain 1750–1900
   ■ The Twentieth-Century World 1900 to the present.

2. Select three pictures from the picture pack of your chosen period which show why this period was a good time to be alive.

3. Use them to explain in your own words why YOU would like to have lived during that particular period.

I chose to live in _____ period

I chose Picture Source _____ because:

_____

_____

_____

I chose Picture Source _____ because:

_____

_____

_____

I chose Picture Source _____ because:

_____

_____

_____

© JOHN MURRAY   *THE TWENTIETH-CENTURY WORLD SUPPORT MATERIALS*   **223**

44

Your task

You should work on your own for this task.

1. Decide which of the four periods you would least like to live in.
2. Select three pictures from the picture pack of your chosen period which show why this period was a bad time to be alive.
3. Use them to explain in your own words why YOU would NOT like to have lived during that particular period.

I chose not to live in _____ period.

I chose Picture Source _____ because:

_____

_____

_____

I chose Picture Source _____ because:

_____

_____

_____

I chose Picture Source _____ because:

_____

_____

_____

45

You will need
- one of the picture packs
- pen or pencil

Comparing periods: 1066 to the present

Your task

Your teacher will divide the class into eight different groups. There will be two groups for each picture pack.

Group A lists all the pros of living in medieval times.
Group B lists all the cons of living in medieval times.

Group C lists all the pros of living in Tudor and Stuart times.
Group D lists all the cons of living in Tudor and Stuart times.

Group E lists all the pros of living in Industrial Revolution times.
Group F lists all the cons of living in Industrial Revolution times.

Group G lists all the pros of living in twentieth-century times.
Group H lists all the cons of living in twentieth-century times.

1. Which group has the longest list?

_____

2. Are there any threads running through the pros or the cons? For example, is the threat of violence a 'con' for all four periods?

_____

_____

_____

_____

_____

> Which do you think was the best period to be born in? Make sure you have evidence to support your viewpoint.

History Dictionary

alliance
an agreement between two countries to help each other. Sometimes this involves helping each other to fight against other countries

Allies
Britain, France, the USA and other countries who joined together to fight against Germany, Italy and Japan in the Second World War

anti-Semitism
persecuting or **discriminating** against **Jews**

atomic bomb
a powerful bomb invented during the Second World War. The Americans ended the War by dropping two atomic bombs on Japan. See **nuclear missiles**

Blitz
heavy night-time bombing of Britain's cities by the German air force in 1940–41

campaign
an organised course of action for a particular purpose. For example, the Suffragettes campaigned to win public support for giving women the **vote**

causes (long-term and short-term)
the reasons why an event takes place. Long-term causes build up slowly over many years. Short-term causes are more like a trigger which finally make things happen

Chancellor
the head of the German **government**

Christians
followers of Jesus Christ, members of one of the Christian churches, for example Catholics or Protestants

civilians
people who are not part of the army

communications
the ways that information is spread to people, for example newspapers, television, radio

Communism
a system of government introduced in Russia after the Revolution in 1917. Key features: all land, industry and business belonged to the state, not private individuals. A strong government controlled all aspects of everyday life. Political opposition was not allowed

concentration camp
a prison camp where the Nazis sent **Jews**, gypsies, political opponents and other people they wanted to get rid of. Millions were killed in the concentration camps

democracy
a system of **government** where everyone has a say in which political party runs the country by voting in elections

dictatorship
a system of **government** where a strong leader (the dictator) has all the power. Communists, Fascists and Nazis believed dictatorship was the best system of government

discovery
when someone finds out or **invents** something new

discrimination
treating a person unfairly, for example because of their race or religion

Edwardian
the period of British history (1900–1914) leading up to the First World War.

election
the process of choosing a **government** by **voting**

evacuation
sending children from towns to the country during the Second World War, for their safety

extremist
someone with a very strong set of political beliefs. Extremists often try to make other people accept they views, by any means possible

eyewitness
a person who is present at an event and can give information about it afterwards

Fascism
the system of government introduced by Mussolini and the Fascist Party in Italy in the 1920s. Key features: strong leadership by a dictator (Mussolini), crushing political opposition, controlling everyday life, making Italy strong and powerful, racist beliefs

generation
each step in a family tree – there are around 30 years between each different generation

ghetto
an area of a city where **Jews** had to live

government
the people who are in charge of running a country. Different countries have different 'systems of government'. See **democracy** and **dictatorship**

Great War
another name for the First World War (1914–1918)

Holocaust
the murder of millions of **Jews** by the Nazis during the Second World War

inflation
when prices rise

invention
a new machine

Jew

a member of the race descended from the ancient Israelites. Jews are now living throughout the world, but are linked by their religion and traditions

League of Nations

an organisation set up after the First World War. It was joined by many countries from all over the world. The purpose of the League was to try to prevent another war by solving disagreements peacefully

morale

the state of people's confidence in their country, leaders or army

Nazism

the type of **government** introduced by Hitler and the Nazi Party in Germany in the 1930s. Key features: strong leadership by a dictator (Hitler), crushing political opposition, controlling everyday life, making Germany strong and powerful, racist beliefs (Hitler said the best Germans were fair-skinned, blue-eyed and blond-haired). Jews and other groups were persecuted and murdered

nuclear

energy created when the nuclei of atoms are forced together. It can be used in bombs and weapons

Nuremberg Laws

anti-Jewish laws introduced by the Nazis in 1935

occupation

when one country's forces take over and run another country

persecution

treating a person badly, for example because of race or religion

President

the head of state in Germany. The President appointed the Chancellor to run the day-to-day affairs of government. Hitler held both posts from 1934 onwards

Prime Minister

the head of the elected government

propaganda

information produced by a group or political party to win more support for themselves, or to persuade people not to support another group

rationing

allowing people only a certain amount of particular foods or other products, especially during a war when supplies are limited

Suffragette

a woman who tried to win the **vote** for women. Suffragettes were willing to break the law to get the **government** to listen to them

suffragist

a person who believes that all adults should be given the right to **vote**. Early in the twentieth century suffragists began to **campaign** to win the **vote** for women. They used peaceful means

surrender

to give yourself up or, for an army, to admit you have lost a battle or a war

synagogue

a Jewish place of worship

technology

new machines and methods developed as a result of scientific research

treaty

an agreement made between people or countries. They each promise to do certain things

trench warfare

war carried on from long, deep ditches known as trenches. This kind of warfare took place during the First World War

unemployment

not having any paid work

vote

take part in an **election**

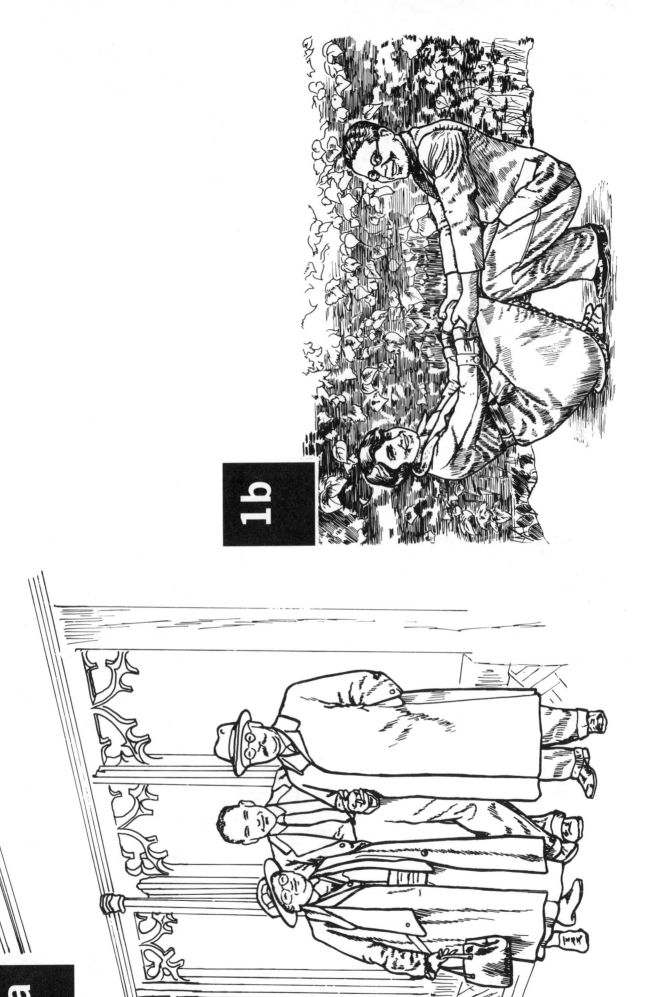

1b

1a

THE TWENTIETH-CENTURY WORLD SUPPORT MATERIALS © JOHN MURRAY

3a

3b

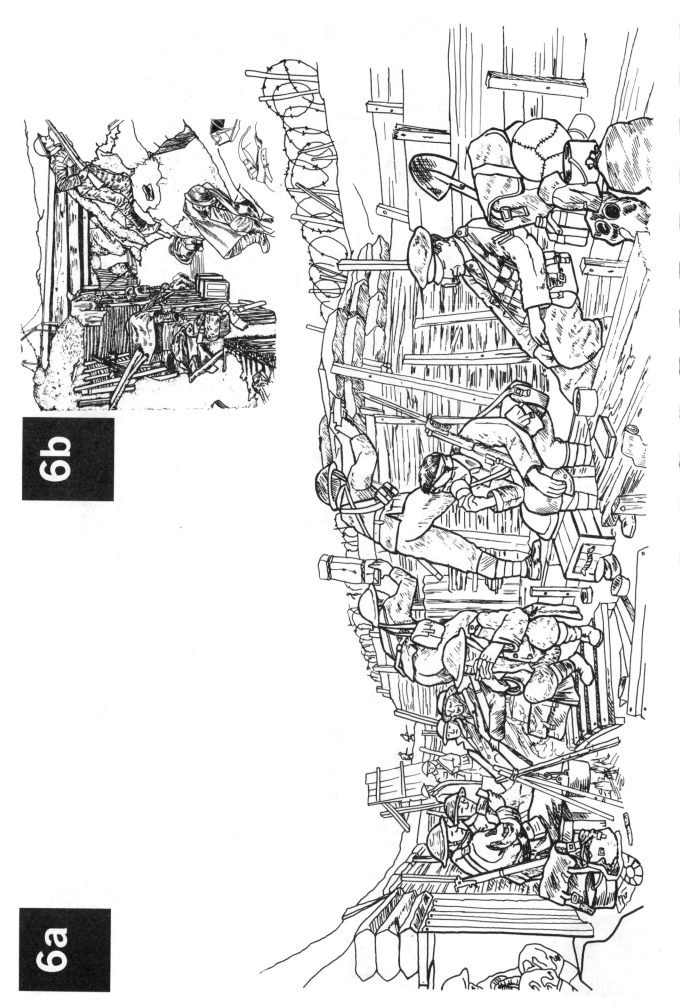

6b

6a

THE TWENTIETH-CENTURY WORLD SUPPORT MATERIALS © JOHN MURRAY

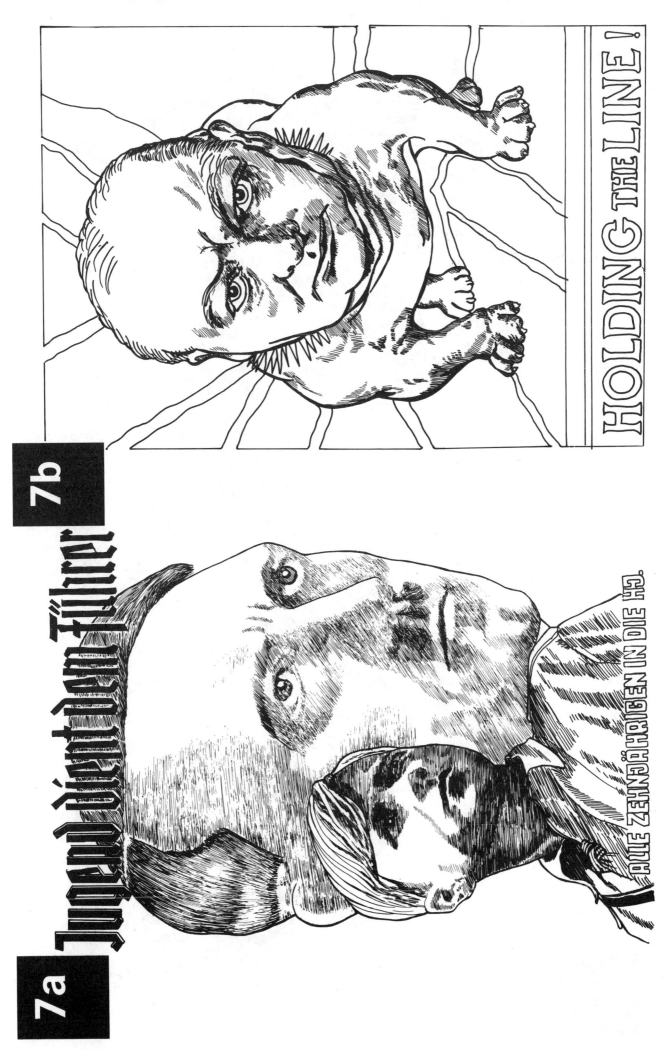

7b HOLDING THE LINE!

7a Jugend dient dem Führer

ALLE ZEHNJÄHRIGEN IN DIE CH.

THE TWENTIETH-CENTURY WORLD SUPPORT MATERIALS © JOHN MURRAY

9a

9b

10b

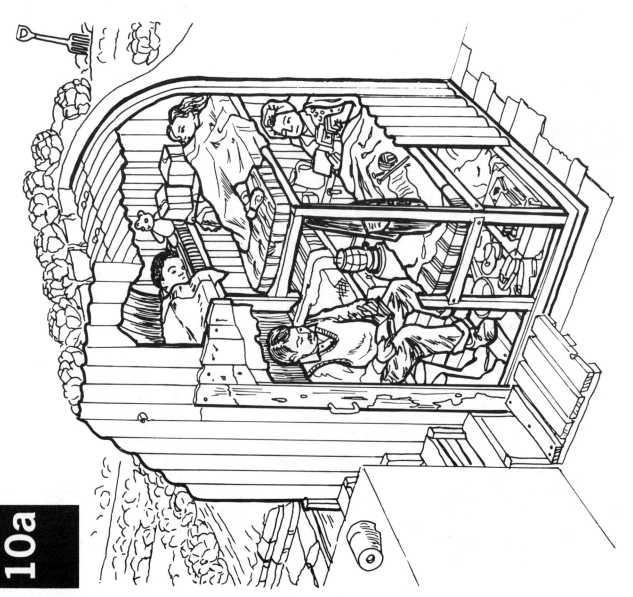

10a

THE TWENTIETH-CENTURY WORLD SUPPORT MATERIALS © JOHN MURRAY

11

DAIRIES

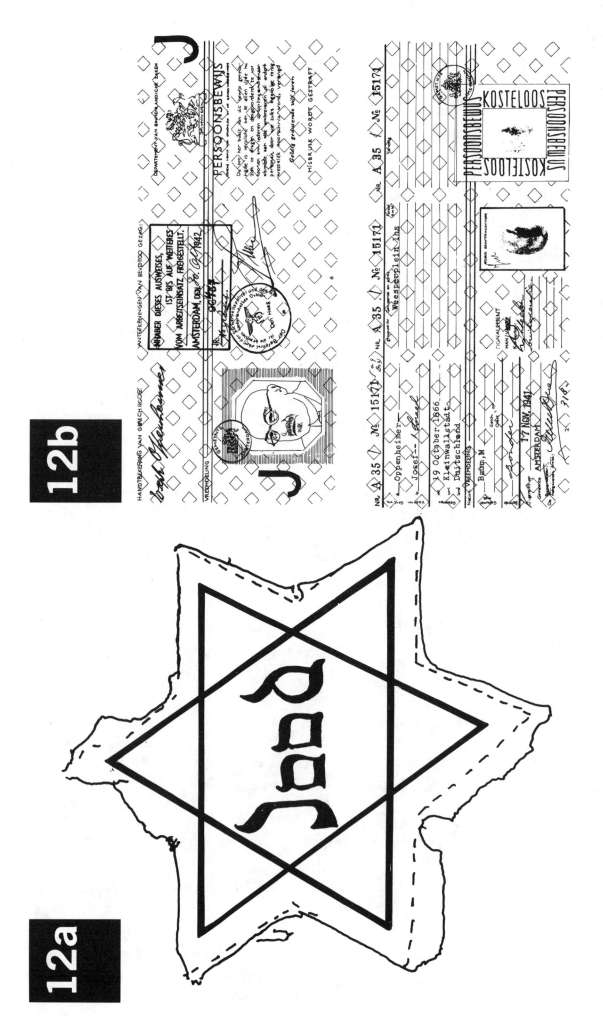

12b

12a

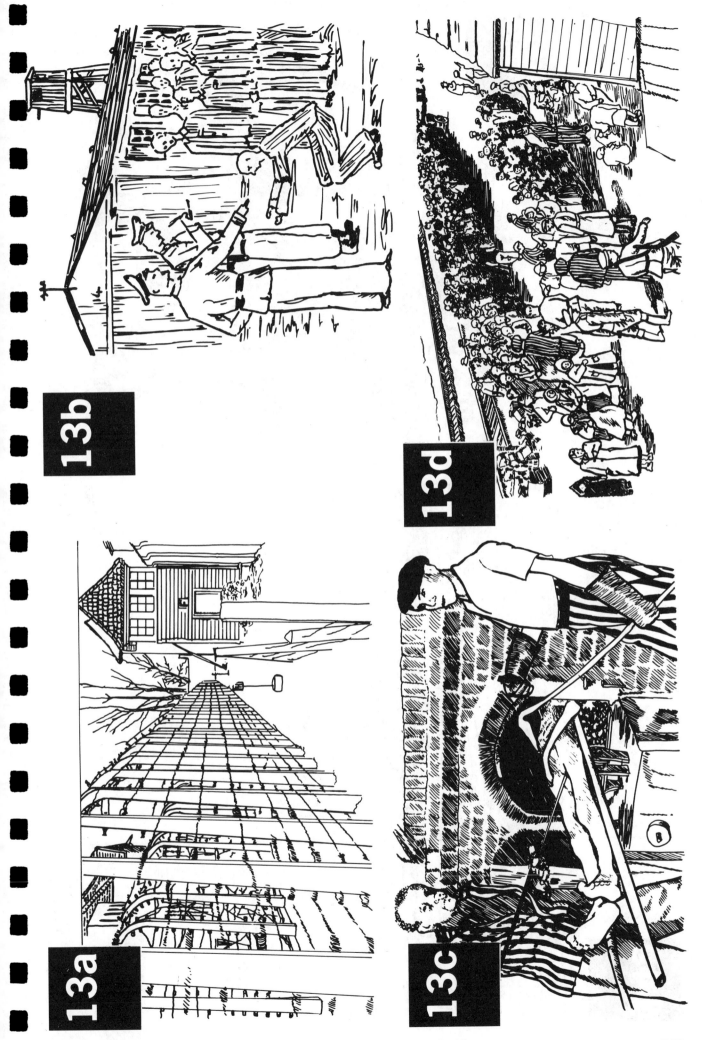

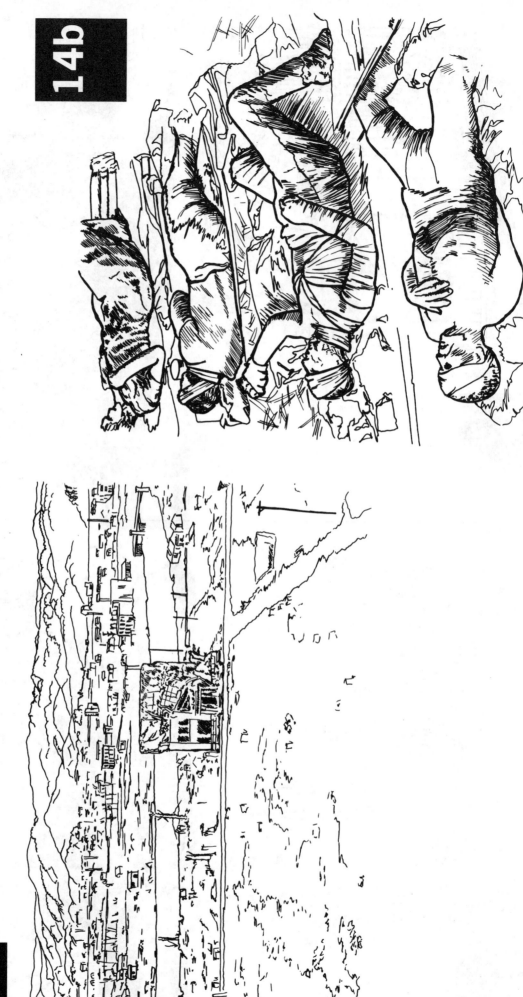

14b

14a

THE TWENTIETH-CENTURY WORLD SUPPORT MATERIALS © JOHN MURRAY

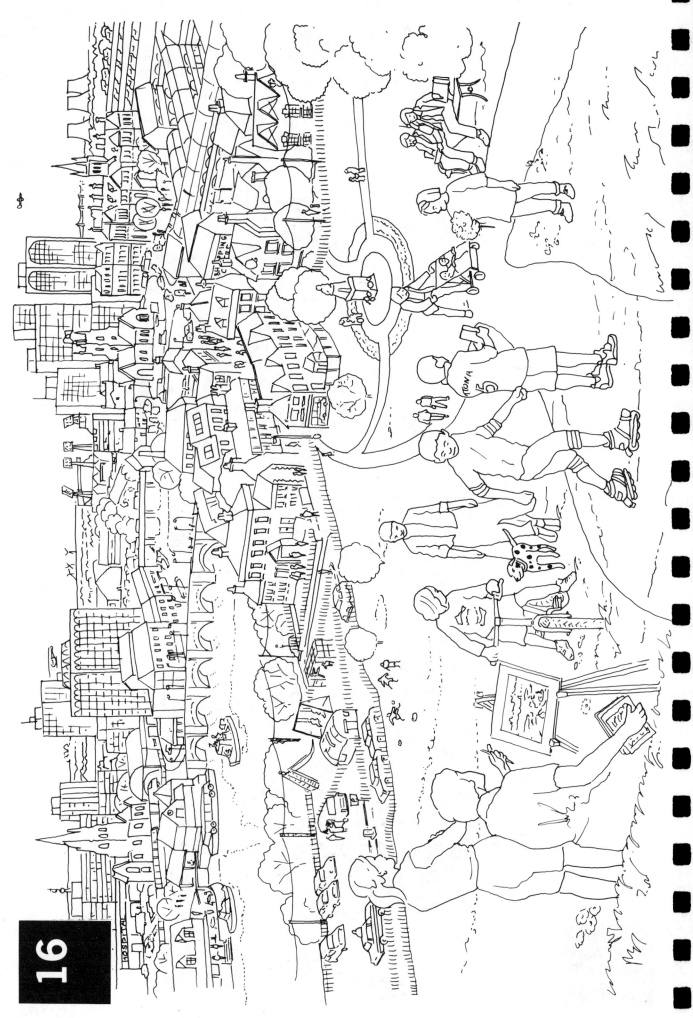

THE TWENTIETH-CENTURY WORLD SUPPORT MATERIALS © JOHN MURRAY